# French Family Cooking

**Margaret Leeming**

**Macdonald Guidelines**

**Editorial manager**
Chester Fisher
**Series editor**
Jim Miles
**Editor**
Neil Tennant
**Designer**
Camron
**Picture researcher**
Jenny de Gex
**Production**
Penny Kitchenham

Made and printed by
Waterlow (Dunstable) Limited

**ISBN 0 356 06436 0**
(cased edition)
**ISBN 0 356 06036 5**
(paperback edition)

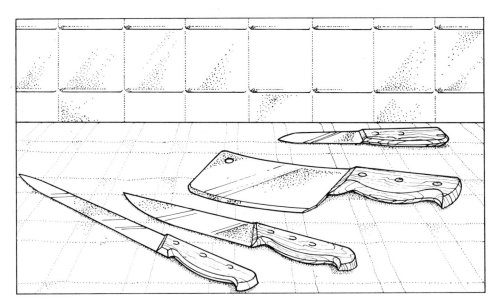

# Contents

© Macdonald Educational Ltd 1979
First published 1979
Macdonald Educational Ltd,
Holywell House, Worship Street,
London EC2A 2EN

# Food and the French

Good food and France are synonymous. Evidence of this lies not just in the tradition of French *haute cuisine*, which is practised and appreciated in almost every important hotel and restaurant the world over, but in the simple cooking of the small provincial restaurants and *auberges* found all over France, and in ordinary French homes. The recipes in this book are typical of the sort of cooking practised by French housewives, most of whom would have some acquaintance with all the dishes described.

In France, food is treated with respect, and at every level of French life there is an innate understanding and appreciation of food and its characteristics. This understanding is shown by the knowledge and skill that the French display in choosing and judging the wide variety of French cheeses that are on sale throughout the country.

The French talk without affectation about the foods they eat and the wines that go with them. In the evenings and at week-ends the hypermarkets are crowded with couples choosing food together. The ability to cook is a skill and a craft which people— both men and women—are proud to possess. French housewives, even those with jobs outside the home, delight in the style of their meals. A tradition of care and skill in the preparation of food is handed down by example from mother to daughter. Moreover, Frenchwomen expect to know how to *construct* a meal, just as they know how to choose vegetables and meat.

▶ An open-air market in Aix-en-Provence

## The choice of food

The interest in food and its importance in everyday life is reflected in the quality and range of the foods available in France. Even convenience foods, which are becoming increasingly popular, are represented by a range of immense variety and sophistication, giving a choice that would be inconceivable to housewives in many other countries. Such choice exists not only in the hypermarkets but in the groceries of small towns and large villages. In the field of traditional, ready-prepared foods such as cooked meats and pastries, standard items in French meals, even a small-town *charcutier* may stock up to twenty different kinds of cooked meats and other savoury dishes, such as *ballotines*, pâtés and terrines, *rillettes*, *andouilles*, sausages and locally cured hams as well as prepared dishes like eggs in aspic or quiches. The small-town baker may have six or seven different types of freshly baked bread, often baked on the premises, although it is becoming harder, even in France, to find

▲ Fresh, natural foods are the basis of the best French cooking, both in the home and in good restaurants.

the traditional country breads such as rye and wholemeal. The local *pâtissier* in the same small town will have an extensive range of open fruit tarts and freshly made traditional pastries as well as local delicacies and various types of homemade sweets.

Most small towns have a market once a week. Much of the local produce on sale will have been brought in by the producers themselves—mounds of fresh garlic, seasonal vegetables of all kinds, eggs, fruit and various kinds of edible fungi. Some farmers' wives will bring in regional specialities such as cakes they have made themselves, their own freshly killed poultry, or cream and cheese made from their own cows' or goats' milk. Other market stalls will be devoted to various kinds of olives and pickles, such as gherkins and peppers preserved in olive oil. There will

also be an astonishing choice of fish, all laid out on blocks of ice to keep it fresh, even at markets well inland, and probably stalls selling dried cod too.

Non-local produce may be in evidence, too, where travelling shops specializing in, for example, cheeses or cooked meats, have set up stalls for the day. Butchers will have done the same, while elsewhere live rabbits, ducks, chickens and snails will be on sale to discerning customers.

## French family meals

A French family will start the day with *petit déjeuner*, or breakfast, which is regarded mainly as a snack. It will consist of milky coffee, drunk from large cups or bowls, sometimes with a spoon, and bread —bought that day if the family lives close to a bakery—spread with butter and jam and balanced on a saucer. Most families do not have croissants for breakfast except at weekends or holiday times. Nowadays, as more women go out to work, English-type pan loaves, which can be kept for several days, are often bought to make into toast for breakfast.

The main meal (*dîner*) is eaten in the middle of the day, either at home or in a restaurant or canteen. Like the rest of the Western world, the French have become very aware of cholesterol and the dangers of over-eating. So the main meal comprises an hors-d'oeuvre or soup, a meat dish with perhaps a separate course of either vegetables or green salad and, finally, either a dessert or fruit or cheese. The evening meal (*souper*) will be lighter: soup or an hors-d'oeuvre, a fish, cheese or egg dish, then fruit or cheese or a fruit-flavoured yoghurt.

If entertaining visitors, there may be a *plat unique*, a dish such as *cous-cous* or *paella* that is complete in itself, or the meal may be more traditional, with four or five courses. Nowadays, many families claim to seldom drink wine except when entertaining, on which occasions they would expect to serve one labelled '*VDQS*' (*vin délimité de qualité supérieure*) or '*appellation contrôlée*'.

# France–a cook's tour

As one travels in France it is impossible not to be impressed by the sheer size and scale of the countryside, and by the ability of France to resemble her neighbours and yet remain completely French.

In the north of France, in Artois, close to the Belgian border, the villages seem curiously unstylish with few flowers or gardens. This is a beer-drinking area and the restaurants are few and far between. Further east on the German border is Alsace-Lorraine, an area famous for its pork-based *charcuterie*, freshwater fish and Strasbourg geese. Mirabelle plums and cherries match the light Alsatian wines such as Sylvaner and Riesling.

To the south-west of Alsace lies Burgundy, arguably the gastronomic heart of France, from where come some of the greatest French wines, such as Chablis, Côtes de Nuits, Beaune, Mâcon and Beaujolais. Burgundy's secure and settled countryside, with its pepperpot farm towers, produces an enormous wealth of foods—chickens from Bresse, beef and game, freshwater fish, snails and various mushrooms and edible fungi.

Provence, in the far south-east of France, has a very different culinary style and landscape. Big farms or *maas* and their attendant cottages make up the hamlets, with dark cypresses marking the farmsteads and graveyards. The flavour of the food is Italian-influenced, with plenty of fish, garlic, black olives and olive oil, but also with the subtle herbs, such as thyme, bay and parsley, that grow wild in the countryside of the Midi and mark the food as French.

Further west along the Mediterranean coast is Languedoc, famous for dishes made with the produce of the region: fish soups from Sète and Montpellier at the coast, and, from the west, the *cassoulets* of Toulouse and Carcassone. Inland also there are the sheep from whose milk cheese is made, notably Roquefort. The harsh, stony land of the Garrique is perfumed with wild herbs, and the snails, rabbits and other game that live there have a particularly delicate flesh. Everywhere in the south there are vineyards. From these comes the basic French *vin ordinaire* which, though it may not excite the connoisseur, is very pleasant to drink.

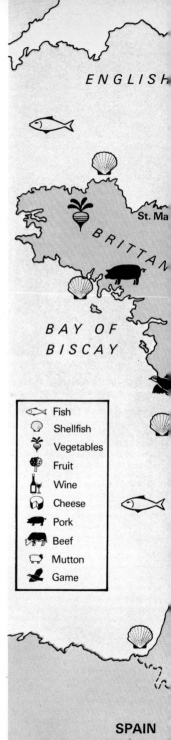

ENGLISH

St. Ma

BRITTANY

BAY OF BISCAY

Fish
Shellfish
Vegetables
Fruit
Wine
Cheese
Pork
Beef
Mutton
Game

SPAIN

## The West

Along the Spanish frontier in the Basque land there is a curious fusion of Spanish and French. The sports page of the local paper features a column on bullfighting. The food is full of sweet peppers, but they are cooked in lard or goose fat and one of the most famous foods of the region is the Bayonne ham, a sweet cured ham that can be eaten thinly sliced and raw or cut into thicker slices and fried.

Further north in the west of France is the wine-growing area of Bordeaux, from where come Sauternes and the great clarets such as Médoc, and also Armagnac brandy. Here, between Aquitaine and Poitou, is the Dordogne, a region of wild landscapes with steep gorges and soaring wooded heights, where every *charcutier* has his own *confit d'oie*, game pâtés and potted truffles.

In contrast to the Dordogne is the Loire valley with its châteaux, wide river and harmonious landscape. This is the home of the light Anjou wines, among them Muscadet and Vouvray. From the Loire valley come the freshwater fish—salmon, tench and bream—for which this region is famous.

Along the northern coast lie Brittany and Normandy with their fish and shellfish. Normandy is also a land of milk and cream and of cheeses such as Camembert and Pont l'Évêque. The cows graze in orchards of apples from which are made cider and Calvados. Normandy also has an unparalleled reputation for *charcuterie*.

◀ Every town in France has its own market selling a wide range of local produce. The photographs to the left show markets in the Dordogne region (*top*), Clermont L'Hérault in Languedoc (*middle*) and Brittany (*bottom*).

# Basic ingredients

Most of the ingredients in French cooking are familiar to other European cooks and need no explanation. However, there are a few basic ingredients, like butter, olive oil and wine, which, while known everywhere, have a particular place in French cooking that may be unfamiliar to some people.

## Seasonings

The bouquet garni is one of the commonest ingredients of savoury dishes in France. It is made of parsley, thyme and a bay leaf with the addition of a clove of garlic or a small stick of celery as desired. Bouquets garnis can be bought ready made, but they are very simple to make (see photograph, right), and assembling your own provides an opportunity for varying the size and contents for individual dishes. Bouquets garnis should be removed before the dish is served.

▲ Tying a bouquet garni—parsley, thyme and a bay leaf—with cotton.

▼ Ingredients for *fines herbes*—parsley, tarragon and chives—used in vinaigrette dressings and in omelettes.

11

Parsley can be bought fresh throughout the year. Thyme can be dried in branches in the summer and stored in a dry place; even the stalks retain the flavour. Bay leaves can easily be bought dried. All of these can be grown in the garden. These are the commonest herbs in French cooking, but many others are also used, such as tarragon, marjoram, chives, rosemary, juniper berries and fennel. Parsley is often chopped and used as a garnish.

Shallots, as well as onions, are common ingredients in French recipes. They have a relatively strong flavour for their size, and are considered more digestible than onions because they break down in cooking. They cannot often be found at English greengrocers, but can be grown from either seeds or sets.

The French have a form of sea salt which is coarse in texture but has a sharp, spicy flavour of its own, compared with the standard, highly refined table salt. It can be milled in a salt mill similar to a pepper mill. In France, it is normal to grind both black and white pepper freshly when it is required. White pepper is stronger and hotter than black, which is more aromatic. A French spice called *quatre-épices* is often used in cooked-meat dishes such as pâtés. It is a mixture of pepper, cloves, ginger and nutmeg, and is not easy to find outside France. Mixed spice is sweeter and includes cinnamon but no pepper. However, it can be used as a substitute.

## Fats

The fat which goes into a dish makes an important contribution to its final flavour. In France, each region tends to cook with the local produce, which helps give identifying flavours to French regional cooking. So in Périgord, for example, many dishes are cooked with goose fat; this can be bought in specialist food shops outside France. In the south, near the Mediterranean, olive oil is the identifying flavour; in the east, it is lard.

Butter is used frequently in both meat and vegetable dishes. The French consider the special flavour that butter gives to a dish is well worth the extra cost, and indeed many recipes are pale shadows of themselves if margarine is substituted for butter.

Olive oil, which gives a characteristic aroma to southern cooking, comes in varying qualities and at varying prices. The *extra vierge* or first pressing should be used for salad dressings, while the cheaper varieties can be used for cooking.

## Pork fat and bacon

Pork fat is used in many different ways in French cooking. The hard back fat which comes from just under the skin can be beaten out and used as a lining for a pâté tin, or cut into strips and used for larding.

The skin itself can be diced or used as a piece and added to various stews and meat dishes to give extra richness. The fat from inside the pig can be rendered down with a little water in a low oven and used for frying. Many French cooks add a small quantity of belly of pork, either fresh or salted, to their stews and braises. Since it can be difficult to buy salt pork, fat streaky bacon, either smoked or plain, can be substituted; but it must be simmered in water for fifteen minutes to remove the bacon taste before being used or the whole dish will taste of nothing but bacon. Buy the bacon in a thick slice, rather than in rashers.

The French have many varieties of locally cured hams, some of which, like Bayonne ham, are eaten raw in thin slices as part of an hors-d'oeuvre, while others, more like English ham, require cooking and are used in a variety of dishes.

▼ Making pâté the traditional way at home.

# Wine and vinegar

Low-quality wine can be bought very cheaply in French supermarkets. To the French cook, wine is not a luxury but a commonplace, like stock, and it is essential in some French dishes if an authentic flavour is to be achieved. The wine is always cooked with the food, and not just added at the end as a flavouring. The better the wine, the better the dish, but indifferent wine is better than none. The last glass of good wine left in a bottle can be used for cooking even after being kept, in a cool place, for some weeks. It is also possible in emergencies to use a very little wine vinegar instead—about 10 ml (1 dessertspoon) vinegar for 100 ml of wine. It is not as good but it is better than nothing, especially for fish.

Meat or poultry which has been fried is often flambéd with brandy or other spirits before the sauce is added. This operation burns off both the alcohol and any remaining film of fat on the meat but leaves the flavour.

Spirits and liqueurs are used in flavouring some dishes, particularly desserts, but care should always be taken not to overdo the quantities—food smothered in alcohol is not particularly good to eat and is not authentic French cooking.

Where vinegar is called for, the French always use wine vinegar, not malt vinegar. It has a delicate flavour which blends well with herbs.

# Cream and cheese

Cream appears in most types of French dishes, not just desserts. It is part of the attention to the finishing of a dish which is one characteristic of French cooking. To leave cream out of a recipe often leaves the dish tasting incomplete. Cream in soups and sauces should not be cooked, but added at the end of the cooking and just warmed. It is apt to curdle or lose its texture if boiled.

The normal hard-grating cheese in French cooking is Gruyère. It should always be grated freshly before use. Cheddar or Lancashire cheese is a perfectly acceptable substitute in many recipes. Local French varieties such as Cantal are used in regional dishes in France. The French also use various kinds of fresh cheeses, akin to cottage and cream cheese. *Petit Suisse* is a cream cheese that is used in both savoury and sweet dishes. It is sold in

**Sorrel**

**Chicory**

**Endive**

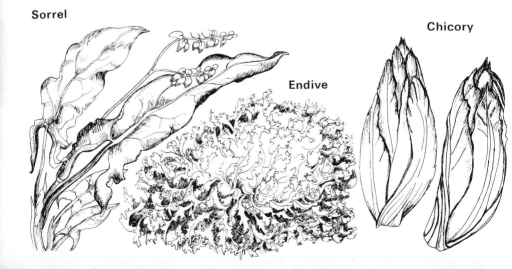

many supermarkets. Alternatively, a plain cream cheese can be substituted. A variety of unsalted cream cheese (*fromage blanc*) is eaten as a dessert in France with sugar and cream.

## Unusual vegetables

Artichokes are a highly developed kind of thistle with an edible flower head. The 'choke' is the silky, under-developed flower that is removed before its fleshy succulent base is eaten. The fleshy base of each leaf (sepal) on the flower head is also edible. The tiny Italian artichokes are eaten whole. Artichokes are boiled and eaten cold as an hors-d'oeuvre or as a separate vegetable.

Fennel is a greenish bulb with a slightly aniseed flavour. It can be eaten raw, finely sliced with a vinaigrette sauce as an hors-d'oeuvre, or cooked as a vegetable. Its leaves can be used as a herb, either fresh or dried, especially with fish.

Celeriac has an edible stem base, shaped like a turnip. (The stalks, unlike those of common celery, are inedible.) Celeriac can be grated and eaten raw as part of an hors-d'oeuvre or it can be cooked and used as a vegetable or in soups.

Pumpkins are large round gourds. The bright orange flesh, with the seeds and peel removed, can be used in soups or as a vegetable.

Sorrel looks rather like spinach and is often cooked with spinach or in its place. Some varieties are very bitter and need blanching for about five minutes in a lot of boiling water, to remove the excess acidity, before being used.

Chicory (*endive* in French) should never be washed but just wiped. Any damaged leaves should be removed. It can be eaten raw as an hors-d'oeuvre with a vinaigrette sauce or cooked as a vegetable.

Endive (*chicorée* in French) looks rather like a yellowish-green mop-head with thin, curled leaves. If it is young and pale it can be eaten as a salad, but if it is dark green it is apt to be bitter, and it is better to blanch it and then cook it like spinach or use it for soup.

Small white onions like large round spring onions can be bought in France, but are not very common elsewhere. In many cases an ordinary onion, quartered, makes an acceptable substitute, though it will not look so good. However, where the recipe calls for glazed onions, it is best to try to find small pickling onions.

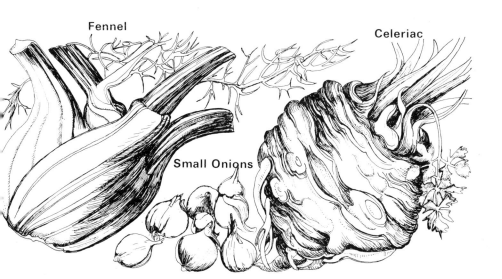

Fennel

Celeriac

Small Onions

## Bread

French bread has a well-deserved reputation for excellence. The French housewife buys freshly baked bread each day, because the standard loaves from French bakeries do not keep well. Today, no French housewife would dream of making her own bread, although this was not so at the turn of the century. In some rural areas, for example, everyone would make their own *pain de campagne* about once a week. Once the oven was lit, a child would be sent out to the neighbours to find who had made bread the day before and so collect some fresh dough-starter—there was no yeast on sale in those days.

Nowadays people normally buy long loaves of white bread: *baguettes* weighing 250 g ($\frac{1}{2}$ lb), *gros pains* of 400 g (14 oz) and *flûtes* or *ficelles* of 100 g (4 oz). The taste and quality of the bread varies from good to better, depending on the baker. *Pain de campagne* is now made by bakers, in either large long loaves or round ones weighing about 1 kg (2 lb). It is a coarse bread that improves with keeping and has a fermented, winey taste.

In some bakers' shops it is also possible to buy *pain de seigle*, rye bread made into flat round loaves, or *pain complet*, a brownish-grey loaf of wholemeal flour. The baker will also make *brioches*, buns made with an egg-enriched dough, and *croissants*, delicate crescents of puff-pastry dough.

## Dried vegetables

Haricot beans are white dried beans. They need soaking before they can be used; the length of soaking depends partly on their age, but less than 12 hours is rarely adequate. They should then always be rinsed. They are used in soups and in meat dishes.

Chick peas are cream-coloured peas which are bought dried. They must be soaked before being used in salads, soups or stews.

The French varieties of lentil are brown or green, not orange. Lentils can be used in soups and in some vegetable dishes. They do not require soaking before use.

# Hors-d'oeuvres

Almost all family dinners in France start with some kind of soup or hors-d'oeuvre. The latter may consist of just one vegetable in a vinaigrette dressing or a collection of different vegetables all with separate dressings. A few slices of pâté, sliced raw ham, French sausage or rillettes could be included, or fish or hard-boiled eggs in mayonnaise. Olives or gherkins are other common items. This first course, served in separate bowls or arranged on one big plate, is quite as important as the main course and should tempt and encourage the diner, not overwhelm him.

In France, pâtés and *rillettes* are bought at the local *charcuterie*, where they are often made to the owner's own recipes. The French housewife does not expect to make her own.

A *plat de crudités* would consist of various cooked and uncooked vegetables, often including beetroot but with no meat or fish. French bread always accompanies the hors-d'oeuvre. Some dishes, such as *salade niçoise*, are considered to be a complete hors'd'oeuvre in themselves.

## Raw vegetable salads

**Radishes** Wash in cold water and cut off the roots. Leave about 2 cm (1 in) of stalk on the other end. Serve without a dressing.

**Tomatoes** Slice on to a serving dish and sprinkle with chopped parsley (about 5 ml/1 teaspoon to each tomato). Pour a well-seasoned vinaigrette dressing over and serve.

**Carrots** Wash, grate finely, then dress with the juice of half a lemon mixed with 30 ml (2 tablespoons) oil, salt and pepper, and sprinkle with chopped chives.

**Cucumbers** Wash and cut into thin slices. Do not peel. Sprinkle with salt and leave for about 2 hours. Drain. If they seem salty, rinse under a cold tap. Dress with oil and freshly ground black pepper, or with a vinaigrette dressing.

**Cauliflower** Wash and break into small florets and serve in a well-seasoned mayonnaise. Leave in the

mayonnaise for 1 hour before serving.

**Celeriac** Peel, grate coarsely and soak in a little oil and vinegar to keep white. Make a sauce of French mustard and oil, seasoned with freshly ground black pepper, and mix with the celeriac before serving.

## Cooked vegetable salads

**Peppers** De-seed, slice thinly and cook for 5 minutes in boiling, salted water. Drain and leave to cool, then serve in a vinaigrette dressing. *Or* put the peppers under a hot grill and turn them frequently so that the skin is evenly blistered. Then peel, remove the seeds, slice and serve in a vinaigrette dressing.

**Beetroot** Boil, peel, allow to cool. Serve diced in a vinaigrette dressing with chopped chives and parsley.

**Mushrooms** Wipe and, if necessary, peel. Remove the centre stalk and slice. Poach for about 3 minutes in a little butter, then leave to get cold. The mushrooms should still be quite firm. Serve with 30 ml (2 tablespoons) oil to

◀ Mandoline for cutting and slicing vegetables. The blades can be adjusted to cut different thicknesses.

the juice of half a lemon and freshly ground black pepper.

**Cauliflower** Wash and break into florets and put into cold, salted water. Bring to the boil and boil for 3 minutes. Dip immediately into cold water and drain well. Serve in a well-seasoned vinaigrette dressing.

## Hors d'oeuvres recipes

**Note** 'Time' stated at the top of each recipe indicates how far in advance of the meal the cook should start work.

### Salade niçoise

*Time* 25 minutes
*Preparation* 20 minutes
*Serves* 4
250 g (8 oz) French beans
8 tomatoes
1 green pepper
1 small onion (optional)
24 black olives
vinaigrette dressing (p. 70)
lettuce leaves
16 anchovy fillets
4 hard-boiled eggs

Cut the beans into 8-cm (3-in) lengths. Cook in boiling salted water until just soft, then dip quickly in cold water and drain well. Cut the tomatoes into quarters. De-seed the pepper and cut into thin slices. Chop the onion finely and de-stone the olives. Mix all these vegetables together with a well-seasoned vinaigrette dressing. Tear up the lettuce leaves to line individual bowls (not plates) and arrange the dressed vegetables on top. Garnish with the hard-boiled eggs, cut into quarters, and the anchovy fillets.

## Artichoke salad
## (artichauts vinaigrettes)
*Time* 2½ hours
*Preparation* 5 minutes
*Cooking time* 30 minutes
*Serves* 4

4 globe artichokes
1·75 litres (3 pints) cold water
10 ml (2 teaspoons) vinegar
vinaigrette dressing (p. 70)

Trim off the sharp points (if any) at the ends of the artichoke leaves, then put the artichokes with the vinegar into the water. Bring to the boil and boil gently for about 30 minutes. When cooked, the bottom leaf should come away easily if pulled gently. Remove the feathery 'choke' with a spoon and discard. Leave the artichokes upside down to drain and cool. Serve with the vinaigrette dressing.

## Rillettes of pork
## (rillettes de porc)
*Time* 7 hours
*Preparation* 35 minutes
*Cooking time* 5 hours
*Serves* at least 12

750 g (1½ lb) lean pork
500 g (1 lb) pork fat
1 piece pork skin
200 ml (7 fl oz) dry white wine
parsley, thyme and bay leaf
10 ml (2 teaspoons) salt
2·5 ml (½ teaspoon) black pepper
300 ml (½ pint) water

Cut all the meat and fat into pieces, taking care to cut with the grain to retain the meat's long fibres. Put the skin in the bottom of a casserole and then the rest of the ingredients. Do not stint the parsley. Cover and cook in a slow oven (120°C, 225°F/Gas ½) for about 5 hours, by which time the meat should be soft and squash between the fingers. Leave to stand for a short while. Skim off the fat and reserve. Discard the pork skin and bay leaf and, using a fork and spoon or two

forks, tear the meat into shreds. The result should be a stringy mass. Check the seasoning and put the meat into small jars while it is still warm. When cold, melt and pour in the reserved fat to cover the top of each jar. Store in a cool place.

## Terrine of game
## (terrine de gibier)
*Time* 2 days
*Preparation* 30 minutes
*Cooking time* 2 hours
*Serves* 8

at least 180 g (6 oz) of one of the following: cooked venison, hare, rabbit, grouse, pheasant, pigeon (if using uncooked meat, simmer in a little stock until the meat comes off the bone)
up to 600 g (1¼ lb) lean pork
750 g (1½ lb) fat belly pork
45 ml (3 tablespoons) brandy
100 ml (3½ fl oz) dry white wine
35 ml (2 heaped table-spoons) chopped parsley
3 medium eggs

▼ Trim the tips off the artichoke leaves before cooking.

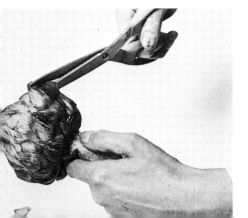

▼ Remove the feathery 'choke' from the centre after cooking.

5 ml (1 teaspoon) *quatre-épices* or mixed spice
10 ml (2 teaspoons) freshly ground black pepper
10 ml (2 teaspoons) salt, or more if necessary
250 g (8 oz) pork fat, in one piece

Cut the game meat off the bones; save a few larger pieces to put in whole. Weigh the rest of the meat and make it up to 750 g (1½ lb) with the lean pork. Mince the game, lean pork and belly together. Mix in the brandy, wine, parsley and beaten eggs. Season well, bearing in mind that seasoning fades with cooking, and leave overnight. Line a large loaf tin or pâté bowl with strips of pork fat beaten out with a wooden spoon until they are very thin, and put in half the minced meat. Lay the reserved pieces of game on top and cover with the remaining mince. Cover with greaseproof paper and tin-foil and bake, standing in a pan of water, in a moderate oven (180°C, 350°F/Gas 4) for 2 hours. Remove the tin-foil and greaseproof paper 30 minutes before the end of cooking. Press while cooling. Serve cold.

▼ Use two forks to tear the cooked pork into shreds for *rillettes.*

## Easter pâté (pâté de Pâques)

*Time* 6 hours
*Preparation* 40 minutes
*Cooking time* 55 minutes
*Serves* 8

250 g (8 oz) shortcrust pastry
350 g (12 oz) lean pork
150 g (6 oz) pork fat
5 ml (1 teaspoon) salt, or more
pepper and cayenne pepper
15 g (½ oz) chopped parsley
egg white
2–3 hard-boiled eggs
beaten egg for glazing

Roll out the pastry to an oblong 28 x 35 cm (11 x 14 in). Mince the meat and fat together and season very well. Mix in the chopped parsley. Paint the pastry with egg white to stop it going soggy and arrange half the meat down one half of the pastry, leaving 2 cm (1 in) clear round the edges. Then lay the hard-boiled eggs down the middle and cover with the rest of the meat. Fold the pastry over and seal the edges very firmly with water. Make a hole in the top for the steam to escape. Glaze with the beaten egg and bake in a hot oven (220°C, 425°F/Gas 7) for 10 minutes and then reduce the heat to 180°C, 350°F/Gas 4 for 45 minutes more. Cover with paper if the top gets too brown. Eat cold, cut into slices.

## Mackerel in white wine (maquereaux marinés au vin blanc)

*Time* 2½ hours
*Preparation* 25 minutes
*Cooking time* 10 minutes
*Serves* 6

2–3 mackerel
2 carrots
1 onion
6 peppercorns
juice of ½ lemon
150 ml (¼ pint) white wine
200 ml (7 fl oz) water
bouquet garni
2 cloves
pinch salt

Ask the fishmonger to fillet the mackerel. Slice the carrots and onion and simmer with all the ingredients except the mackerel for 20 minutes. Strain the stock and poach the mackerel in it very gently for 10 minutes. While still warm, remove their skins and any remaining bones, then return to the cooking liquor to cool. Serve cold in this liquor.

Herrings can be cooked and served in the same way.

20

# Soups

Soup is a normal start to an ordinary meal in France, particularly in the winter. All kinds of vegetables, meat and fish are made into soups, often in very subtle combinations. Sometimes they are thickened with eggs or cream but potatoes, flour, bread, tapioca or ground rice can be used. There is a delicacy and freshness in French soups that, combined with their richness, makes them unforgettable. The Gratinée des Causses below is a good example.

## The use of stock in soups

Stock is used a great deal in French cooking, not just in soups but for cooking vegetables and meat, and in making sauces. Some French soups are based on stock, others on water, although many of the latter taste better if stock is substituted.

There are several methods of obtaining stock. Stock cubes can always be used in emergencies, but their flavour easily becomes familiar and gives everything a uniform taste. A stock for special occasions can be made with fresh meat and bones, particularly veal, but for an ordinary stock chicken bones, either raw or *freshly* cooked, and scraps of meat will do. The stock must not be overcooked. Roast beef and mutton bones do not make good stock. In France, calf's feet provide the jelly in stocks and meat jellies, but pig's trotters can be substituted, as can pork bones and meat for veal.

## Soup recipes
## Basic meat stock
*Time* 3½ hours
*Preparation* 5 minutes
*Cooking time* 1½ hours
500 g (1 lb) veal or lean
   pork and 1 kg (2 lb)
   veal or pork bones *or*
1 chicken carcass and
   chicken scraps
1·75 litres (3 pints) water
1 carrot
1 onion
bouquet garni without
   garlic
salt, pepper
Cut the meat into pieces or

break the chicken bones. Put the meat and bones into a large saucepan with the cold water and bring to the boil. Peel and roughly cut up the vegetables. When the scum starts to rise, skim the top. Turn down the heat so that it is boiling just enough to send up the scum and continue skimming for about 10 minutes until no more appears. Then add the vegetables, bouquet garni, and seasoning and simmer on a low heat for about 1½ hours. Strain, check the seasoning and leave to cool. When cold, skim off the fat.

## Cauliflower soup (potage cancouet)
*Time* 1 hour
*Preparation* 25 minutes
*Cooking time* 35 minutes
*Serves* 4
1 small cauliflower
500 g (1 lb) potatoes
1 lettuce
100 g (4 oz) sliced onion
1 litre (1¾ pints) stock
1 bay leaf
salt, pepper
1 egg yolk
30 ml (2 tablespoons)
   cream
fried croûtons (optional)
Wash and break the cauliflower into small florets. Peel the potatoes and cut them

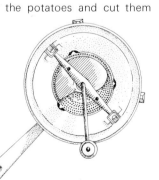

into pieces. Wash and tear the lettuce into strips. Gently poach the lettuce and onion in the butter for 10 minutes and then add the boiling stock, the potatoes, cauliflower and bay leaf. Season and simmer for 15 minutes.

Remove a few pieces of cauliflower to use as garnish later, and continue cooking the soup for another 15 minutes. Liquidize or *mouli* the soup, return it to the pan and re-heat. Check the seasoning. Mix the egg and cream in a heated tureen and pour the soup slowly on to them. Garnish with the reserved cauliflower and serve with hot fried croûtons.

## Simple onion soup (soupe à l'oignon)
*Time* 45 minutes
*Preparation* 15 minutes
*Cooking time* 30 minutes
*Serves* 5
750 g (1½ lb) onions
40 g (1½ oz) butter
15 ml (1 tablespoon) flour
1·25 litres (2 pints) stock
Peel and slice the onions finely. Fry them in the butter in a large saucepan, stirring frequently until they are well browned. Stir in the flour and then gradually add the stock. Simmer for 30 minutes. Serve very hot with grated cheese.

## Fresh pea soup (potage longchamp)
*Time* 1 hour
*Preparation* 25 minutes

◄ *Mouli-légumes* (vegetable mill) used for sieving and making purées.

*Cooking time* 30 minutes
*Serves* 6
2 onions
2 carrots
1 kg (2 lb) fresh peas or
　500 g (1 lb) frozen peas
1 lettuce
1·5 litres (2¼ pints) stock
　or water
bouquet garni
1 mint leaf, chopped
salt, pepper
grated nutmeg
45 ml (3 tablespoons)
　cream

Peel and cut the onions and carrots into pieces. Shell the peas. Wash and tear the lettuce into strips. Put all the vegetables into a saucepan with the stock or water. Bring to the boil, add the bouquet garni, mint, seasoning and nutmeg, cover and simmer for 30 minutes. Put through a sieve or *mouli*, and return to the pan to re-heat. Check the seasoning. Stir in the cream away from the heat just before serving.

### Tomato soup from Périgord (Tourain)

*Time* 1 hour
*Preparation* 15 minutes
*Cooking time* 30 minutes
*Serves* 4
1 litre (1¾ pints) seasoned
　stock or water
180 g (6 oz) onions
1 clove garlic
25 g (1 oz) lard
10 ml (2 teaspoons) flour
500 g (1 lb) tomatoes
1 egg yolk

Boil the stock in a large saucepan. Finely chop the onion and garlic and fry them in the lard. When they are starting to colour, add

the flour and continue cooking for a few minutes. Moisten with about 1 cup of stock and stir well. Then pour this mixture back into the stock. Add the skinned tomatoes, de-seeded and chopped. Leave to cook for 30 minutes. Just before serving, add the egg yolk to thicken. To serve: put slices of toast in a pre-heated soup tureen and pour the soup over them. Serve at once.

### Potato soup (soupe économique)

*Time* 25 minutes
*Preparation* 15 minutes
*Cooking time* 10 minutes
*Serves* 6
500 g (1 lb) potatoes
1·5 litres (2¼ pints) well
　seasoned stock
butter

Peel the potatoes and slice them very finely into the boiling stock. Simmer for 10 minutes, stirring from time to time. Serve very hot with a knob of butter in each bowl.

▼ Egg liaison for soups: add hot soup very gradually to beaten egg yolks and mix well.

### Onion and blue cheese soup (gratinée des Causses)

*Time* 1 hour 20 minutes
*Preparation* 15 minutes
*Cooking time* 1 hour
*Serves* 6
250 g (8 oz) onions
40 g (1½ oz) butter
1¾ litres (3 pints) stock or
　water
salt, pepper
a little grated nutmeg
125 g (5 oz) French bread
100 g (4 oz) Roquefort,
　Stilton or Danish blue
　cheese

Peel and slice the onions finely. Melt the butter in a saucepan and fry the onions very gently, so that they do not brown, for about 5 minutes. Add the stock and season with salt, pepper and nutmeg. Simmer for 5 minutes. Meanwhile, cut the bread into 1-cm (½-in) slices and toast. Then spread thickly with the blue cheese and put into an ovenproof casserole. Pour the soup over and sprinkle the grated

▼ Add beaten egg yolk and cream to the hot soup away from the heat and mix well.

cheese on top. Bake at 190°C, 375°F/Gas 5 for 1 hour. Serve from the bowl in which the dish has been cooked.

## Lettuce soup
## (crème de laitue)
*Time* 1 hour
*Preparation* 10 minutes
*Cooking time* 45 minutes
*Serves* 4
2 lettuces
25 g (1 oz) butter
1 litre (1¾ pints) stock or water
salt, pepper
1 egg yolk
30 ml (2 tablespoons) cream
fried croûtons

Wash and tear up the lettuces. Poach them in the butter until they are soft, and then add the stock and seasoning. Bring to the boil and leave to cook over a very low heat for 45 minutes. Liquidize or *mouli*. Return to the heat and check the seasoning. Stir the egg yolk and cream together in a heated tureen, pour in the soup and serve at once with fried croûtons.

## Pumpkin and haricot bean soup
## (soupe fermière)
*Time* 3 hours + overnight
*Preparation* 25 minutes
*Cooking time* 2½ hours
*Serves* 4
180 g (6 oz) dry haricot beans
1 large clove garlic
1 onion stuck with 2 cloves
1 large bouquet garni, including celery
salt, pepper

1·75 litres (3 pints) good stock, skimmed to remove the fat
500 g (1 lb) pumpkin
15 g (½ oz) butter
45 ml (3 tablespoons) cream
chopped chives for garnish

Soak the haricot beans overnight and then rinse them. Bring them to the boil in a large saucepan with the garlic, onion and cloves, bouquet garni, seasoning and stock. Then turn down the heat and simmer for 1½ hours. Add the pumpkin, peeled, de-seeded and cut into pieces, and continue to simmer for another hour. Then remove the cloves and bouquet garni and sieve or *mouli* the soup. Re-heat and check the seasoning. Melt the butter and mix with the cream in a pre-heated tureen. Pour in the soup and sprinkle the chives on top. Serve at once.

## Cream of chicken soup
## (crème bressane)
*Time* 30 minutes
*Preparation* 20 minutes
*Cooking time* 10 minutes
*Serves* 6
125 g (5 oz) cooked chicken without bones
300 ml (½ pint) Béchamel sauce (p. 83)
50 g (2 oz) boiled rice
1·5 litres (2½ pints) seasoned chicken stock
2 eggs
75 ml (5 tablespoons) cream
salt, pepper
15 ml (1 tablespoon) chopped parsley and chives

Liquidize the chicken,

Béchamel sauce and rice, moistened with a little stock. Reserving 1 cup of stock, add the remainder to the chicken purée and gently bring to the boil. Separate the egg whites and poach them in the reserved stock. When cooked, drain and cut into strips. (Return the stock to the soup.) Mix the egg yolks with the cream and gradually add a little hot soup to the mixture. Then, away from the heat, pour the egg mixture into the soup. Adjust the seasoning. Serve in a heated tureen garnished with the chopped parsley and chives and the strips of egg white.

## Red-cabbage soup
## (soupe au chou-rouge)
## (Flanders)
*Time* 2 hours 15 minutes
*Preparation* 15 minutes
*Cooking time* 2 hours
*Serves* 4
750 g (1½ lb) red cabbage
10 ml (2 teaspoons) vinegar
500 g (1 lb) potatoes
1·25 litres (2 pints) stock
salt, pepper
100 ml (3½ fl oz) red wine
15 g (½ oz) butter

Roughly chop up the cabbage and sprinkle with vinegar to keep it red. Peel and cut the potatoes into pieces and put them in a heavy saucepan with the cabbage. Add the boiling stock and simmer for 2 hours with the pan covered. Season, add the wine and bring to the boil before serving. Serve with a knob of butter in each soup bowl.

# Entrées

At the end of the last century when formal
dinners were gargantuan affairs, the entrée came
after the soup and fish as a prelude to the roast
meats. It usually consisted of a fish or a meat dish
served in its own sauce. Now that the scale on
which we eat has diminished, the entrée as a
course is often omitted. Entrée dishes of dressed
fish, meat or cheese may, however, be served
instead of soup as hot hors-d'oeuvres, or in place
of the fish course. Many of the recipes that follow
may also be served on their own as light supper or
luncheon dishes, perhaps with the quantities
increased. Pictured above (left to right) are
coquilles St Jacques, gougère bourguignonne,
acras, moules farcies and oeufs champenois.

**1**

## RECIPES
### Choux pastry
### *(pâte à choux)*
*Basic recipe*
*Time* 25 minutes
*Preparation* 25 minutes
50 g (2 oz) butter
150 ml ($\frac{1}{4}$ pint) water
pinch salt
65 g ($2\frac{1}{2}$ oz) flour
2 50-g eggs (grade 4)

Put the butter and water with the salt in a saucepan over a low heat and bring slowly to the boil (**1**), allowing all the butter to melt before the water boils. Sift the flour and when the water boils tip it all in at once (**2**). After a moment, remove from the heat and beat hard until the sides and bottom of the pan are clean (**3**). Then add the eggs one at a time and beat vigorously after each has been added (**4**). If the eggs are slightly big, beat the second in a separate bowl and add only sufficient to make a stiff elastic paste—not sticky, but one that will keep its shape. Use as required.

**2**

**3**

**4**

## Fried choux pastry with crab (acras)

*Time* 55 minutes
*Preparation* 35 minutes
*Cooking time* 5 minutes
*Serves* 4

100 g (4 oz) crab meat (to
    dress a crab, see p. 31)
salt, pepper
paprika to taste
choux pastry made with
    2 eggs (p. 26)

Beat the crab to a smooth paste with the seasonings and then beat into the choux pastry. Using two spoons, shape into small balls and drop into very hot deep fat, a few at a time. Fry until golden brown, then drain and keep warm until the rest are cooked. Serve at once with shredded lettuce and a well seasoned vinaigrette dressing or a tomato sauce (p. 87).

## Burgundian cheese pastry (gougère bourguignonne)

*Time* 1 hour 15 minutes
*Preparation* 35 minutes
*Cooking time* 40 minutes
*Serves* 4

choux pastry made with
    2 eggs
black pepper
grated nutmeg
50 g (2 oz) Gruyère or
    Cheddar cheese
egg for glazing

Make the choux pastry and add the pepper and grated nutmeg. Grate half the cheese and beat into the pastry. Using an icing bag, pipe a circle of balls just touching to form a crown on a greased oven sheet. Cut the remaining cheese into ½-cm (¼-in) cubes and dot the pastry ring with these. Glaze with beaten egg, and bake in a hot oven (220°C, 425°F/Gas 7) for 30 minutes. If necessary, reduce the temperature to 190°C, 375°F/Gas 5 after 20 minutes. Then make a series of slits in the sides to allow the steam to escape and the insides to dry. If they remain damp when the gougère cools, it will be soft and tough, not crisp. Return to the oven, turned off, and dry for 10 minutes with the door slightly open. Serve either hot or cold.

## Spinach pasties (chaussons à la florentine)

*Time* 45 minutes
*Preparation* 10 minutes
*Cooking time* 15 minutes
*Serves* 4

2 portions *Petit Suisse* or
    40 g (1½ oz) cream
    cheese
1 egg yolk
15 g (½ oz) grated Gruyère
    or Lancashire cheese
100 g (4 oz) cooked
    spinach, well drained
    and chopped
salt, pepper
350 g (12 oz) bought puff
    pastry

Beat the cream cheese with almost all the egg yolk and the grated cheese. Add the chopped spinach to this mixture and season. Reserve a little egg for glazing the pastry. Roll out the pastry to a thickness of 3 mm (⅛ in). Cut into 8 rounds, 9 cm (3½ in) in diameter. Put some of the cheese and spinach mixture in the centre of each round. Damp the edges and fold into halfmoons. Pinch the edges hard to make a firm seal. Glaze with the reserved egg and cook for 15 minutes in a hot oven (220°C, 425°F/Gas 7).

## Leek quiche (quiche de Saint-Quirin)

*Time* 55 minutes
*Preparation* 25 minutes
*Cooking time* 30 minutes
*Serves* 8

125 g (5 oz) shortcrust
    pastry
500 g (1 lb) leeks (use
    white part only)
30 ml (2 tablespoons)
    cornflour
150 ml (5 oz) milk
2 eggs
30 ml (2 tablespoons)
    cream
75 g (3 oz) grated hard
    cheese
salt, pepper
50 g (2 oz) lean, unsmoked
    bacon

Line an 18-cm (7-in) flan ring with the pastry. Wash the leeks and blanch them in boiling salted water for 5 minutes. Drain well and cut into rounds 1 cm (½ in) thick. Mix the cornflour with the milk and add the beaten eggs, cream, grated cheese, salt and a generous amount of black pepper. Fry the bacon lightly and cut into small dice. Cover the bottom of the flan with the bacon and leeks, spoon the egg mixture over and bake in a hot oven (200°C, 400°F/Gas 6) for 30 minutes. Serve hot or cold.

## Baked eggs with cream (oeufs champenois)

*Time* 20 minutes
*Preparation* 5 minutes
*Cooking time* 10 minutes
*Serves* 4

25 g (1 oz) butter
4 eggs
salt, pepper
30 ml (2 tablespoons) cream

Grease an ovenproof dish with all the butter. Separate the eggs, keeping the yolks whole. Beat the whites until stiff, season with salt and pepper and fold in the cream. Spoon the egg whites into the buttered dish. Make 4 separate holes and drop an egg yolk in each. Bake in a hot oven (220°C, 425°F/ Gas 7) for 10 minutes and serve at once.

## Scallops in white wine (coquilles St Jacques à la parisienne)

*Time* 50 minutes
*Preparation* 30 minutes
*Cooking time* 10 minutes
*Serves* 6

100 ml (3½ fl oz) white wine
bouquet garni
50 g (2 oz) chopped onions
250 g (8 oz) scallops without shells
150 g (6 oz) button mushrooms
40 g (1½ oz) butter
30 ml (2 tablespoons) flour
milk
45 ml (3 tablespoons) cream
6 scallop shells (optional)
Parmesan cheese, grated
breadcrumbs

Put the white wine, onion and bouquet garni in an enamel or non-stick saucepan and simmer for 10 minutes. Add the scallops and cook for another 5 minutes, then remove them from the liquor and put on one side. Strain the liquor and reserve. Wipe the mushrooms and cut any that are large into halves. Poach gently in one-third of the butter for 3 minutes, then drain and add to the scallops.

Make a roux with the remaining butter and flour and moisten with the reserved liquor and enough milk to make a very thick sauce. Remove from the heat and beat in the cream. Mix half of this sauce with the mushrooms and scallops.

Butter the scallop shells, or an ovenproof dish, spoon in the scallops, then cover with the remaining sauce. Sprinkle with Parmesan and breadcrumbs and cook under a hot grill for 10 minutes. Serve at once.

## Stuffed mussels (moules farcies)

*Time* 65 minutes + overnight
*Preparation* 30 minutes
*Cooking time* 10 minutes
*Serves* 6

2 litres (3½ pints) mussels
50 g (2 oz) shallots or onions
3 cloves garlic
30 ml (2 tablespoons) chopped parsley
40 g (1½ oz) softened butter
salt, pepper
50 g (2 oz) breadcrumbs

Prepare the mussels as described on p. 30. Tear the empty shells from the opened mussels and discard. Chop the shallots or onions very finely and crush the garlic. Beat the parsley, garlic. and shallots into the butter, and season the mixture very well. Put a little of this butter on to each mussel, and press it down so it is level with the shell edge. Arrange the mussels in one layer in an ovenproof dish, sprinkle with breadcrumbs and cook in a hot oven (220°C, 425°F/Gas 7) for 10 minutes.

◀ A leek quiche with two *chaussons à la florentine*.

# Fish

In France, fish comes from both the Atlantic and the Mediterranean. The French housewife therefore has a wide range of fish from which to choose, and also a wider choice of freshwater fish and shellfish than is found in many countries. The recipes in this chapter have been chosen, or adapted, for types of fish that are generally available outside France.

A court-bouillon is a wine-and-vegetable-based stock that is used as the cooking liquor for many fish dishes. Here are two basic recipes.

## Court-bouillon
*Time* 35 minutes
*Cooking time* 30 minutes
*Basic recipe I\**
300 ml (½ pint) water
200 ml (7 fl oz) white wine (or red wine in recipes requiring red wine court-bouillon)
1 carrot, sliced
1 onion, sliced
thyme, bay leaf, parsley
salt, 4 peppercorns

*Basic recipe II\**
500 ml (1 pint) water
60 ml (4 tablespoons) wine vinegar
1–2 carrots, cut in rounds
1–2 onions, sliced
1 clove
several stalks of parsley
salt, 4 peppercorns
\*any fish bones, heads or skin can be added to either recipe to increase flavour

Simmer all the ingredients for 30 minutes, then strain before using as directed in the recipes.

## Preparation of mussels
Mussels can be bought frozen without their shells. Frozen mussels can be boiled for 2 minutes with the ingredients specified under the preparation of fresh mussels and then used as directed in the recipes. However, their flavour is not as good as that of fresh mussels.

*Basic recipe*
*Time* 30 minutes + overnight
*Preparation* 30 minutes
*Cooking time* 12 minutes
2 litres (3½ pints) mussels
60 ml (4 tablespoons) Quaker oats
1 medium onion, finely chopped
4 stalks parsley
3–4 peppercorns
1 branch thyme
1 small bay leaf
200 ml (7 fl oz) white wine
200 ml (7 fl oz) water
Put the mussels, sprinkled with porridge oats, in a covered bowl to stand in a cool place overnight; this will both fatten and clean them. The next day, scrub them very thoroughly, changing the water several times, and tear off their beards. *Discard any that are now open.* Put the closed mussels with all the other ingredients in a pan and bring slowly to the boil. Boil fast for 2 minutes, then remove from the heat and strain off the cooking liquor and reserve it. *Throw away any mussels that are now closed.* The mussels are now ready to use.

## Moules marinières
*Time* 35 minutes + overnight
*Preparation* 30 minutes
*Cooking time* 3 minutes
*Serves* 4
2 litres (3½ pints) mussels (prepared as above)
black pepper
45 ml (3 tablespoons) chopped parsley
Put the opened mussels on a heated dish to keep warm.

Return the strained cooking liquor to a clean saucepan and bring to the boil. Check the seasoning and pour the liquor over the mussels. Sprinkle with chopped parsley and serve.

## Mock bouillabaisse (bouillabaisse)
*Time* 1 hour 30 minutes
*Preparation* 1 hour
*Cooking time* 20 minutes
*Serves* 6
1½ kg (3 lb) assorted fish, e.g. haddock, hake steaks, cod steaks, conger eel, skate, whiting, mackerel, sea-bream—as many different kinds as possible
250 g (8 oz) large prawns, unshelled
1 crab
180 g (6 oz) frozen mussels *or* ½ litre (¾ pint) prepared mussels (p. 30)
250 g (8 oz) onions
3 cloves garlic
2 leeks
150 ml (¼ pint) olive oil
250 g (8 oz) ripe tomatoes
bunch of fennel and parsley, *or* parsley + 2·5 ml (½ teaspoon) fennel seeds
1 bay leaf
0·3 g (⅛ teaspoon) saffron finely pared zest of ½ an orange
sea salt, cayenne pepper

Trim and skin the fish, cut it into chunks about 8 x 3 cm (3 x 1 in). Dress the crab (see p. 31). Scrub the small claws well and crack them but leave them whole. Prepare the mussels if necessary (see above). Using all

▶ Never buy a crab without making sure that it is dry inside. To dress a crab, remove all the claws, then tear the centre apron from the main shell. At the point between the two big claws where the apron joins the shell is the mouth. Behind this is a small sac which is the stomach: DISCARD THIS SAC. Around the apron are the feathery gills which are harmless but unsightly. Scrape all the soft brown meat from the shell. Crack the claws and remove all the white meat.

the skin and trimmings but not the mackerel head, make 1·5 litres (2½ pints) vinegar court-bouillon (p. 30). Peel and chop the onions and garlic. Wash and slice the leeks. Skin and roughly chop the tomatoes. Cook the onions, garlic and leeks in the olive oil in a large saucepan, but do not let them brown. Then add the tomatoes, herbs, zest and seasoning. Stir for a few moments, then add the stock and saffron. Boil hard for 4 minutes. Turn down the heat and lay the firm fish, such as cod, haddock, hake and eel, on the vegetables, add more boiling water if necessary to cover, and boil gently for 6–8 minutes. Then add the rest of the fish and the shell fish, including the crab's claws, and boil for another 8–10 minutes. The fish must retain its shape but feel springy to the touch. Check the seasoning. Lay a slice of toasted French bread rubbed with garlic in each pre-heated soup plate. Lift out the pieces of fish first, then ladle out the soup. Serve with grated cheese and chilli - flavoured garlic mayonnaise (see p. 86).

**Crab and vegetable soup (potage Marie-Jeanne)**
*Time* 1 hour
*Preparation* 30 minutes
*Cooking time* 30 minutes
*Serves* 6
2 carrots
3 leeks
2 onions
2 cloves garlic
3 tomatoes
45 ml (3 tablespoons) oil
bouquet garni
1·5 litres (2½ pints) hot water
45 ml (3 tablespoons) ground rice
1 large crab
100 ml (3½ fl oz) cream

Wash, peel and slice the carrots. Wash and cut the leeks into short lengths. Peel and chop the onions and garlic. Skin, de-seed and chop the tomatoes. Fry the carrots, onions and leeks in a large saucepan with the oil. When they start to soften, add the tomatoes, garlic and bouquet garni. Mix well and pour in the hot water mixed with the ground rice. Bring to the boil and simmer for 30 minutes. Meanwhile, dress the crab (see above). When the soup is cooked, liquidize or *mouli* it and return to the pan. Add all the crab meat, check the seasoning and bring back to the boil. Stir in the cream away from the heat and serve hot.

## Sole fried in butter (sole meunière)

*Time* 25 minutes
*Preparation* 5 minutes
*Cooking time* 7–10 minutes each
*Serves* 2 (cooking more than two fish in sequence usually makes the fat too hot, necessitating a clean frying-pan and a fresh quantity of clarified butter)

2 small sole
salt, pepper
milk
flour
100 g (4 oz) clarified butter
15 ml (1 tablespoon) lemon juice
chopped parsley
25 g (1 oz) butter
lemon wedges for garnish

Clean the fish but leave them whole. Season and dip them first in milk and then in flour. Fry them separately in the clarified butter, taking care not to overheat the pan. Turn once, using a big fish slice. Keep the first warm while cooking the second. Serve sprinkled with lemon juice and chopped parsley, and a final splash of fresh butter heated to foaming point. Garnish with lemon wedges.

## Sole with prawns and mushrooms (filets de sole à la normande)

*Time* 1 hour 15 minutes
*Preparation* 35 minutes
*Cooking time* 25 minutes
*Serves* 4

4 soles, filleted and skinned (retain heads, bones and skins)*
100 g (4 oz) button mushrooms
30 ml (2 tablespoons) flour
50 g (2 oz) butter
150 g (6 oz) shelled prawns (well drained if frozen)
60 ml (4 tablespoons) cream
*plaice, which is cheaper, may be substituted

Use the bones, skin and heads of the fish to make a wine *court-bouillon* (p. 30). Wipe and slice the mushrooms, poach them in a little butter for 3 minutes, then put aside. Butter an ovenproof dish and arrange the fillets of fish, folded in halves, on it. Dot with a little butter and pour on enough strained fish stock almost to cover the fish. Cover with tinfoil and bake in the oven (180°C, 350°F/Gas 4) for about 15 minutes, or until the fish is *just* cooked. Then carefully drain off the cooking liquor without disturbing the fish fillets. Make a roux in a saucepan, using half the butter and all the flour, and add 200 ml ($\frac{1}{3}$ pint) of the cooking liquor. Stir well to make a smooth sauce and bring to the boil. Add the mushrooms and prawns, and stir in the cream away from the heat. Check the seasoning. Pour the sauce over the fish and return to the oven (180°C, 350°F/Gas 4) for 5 minutes.

## Haddock poached in white wine (aiglefin à la Dugléré)

*Time* 1 hour 5 minutes
*Preparation* 15 minutes
*Cooking time* 50 minutes
*Serves* 4

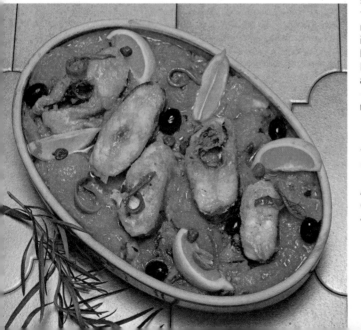

◀ *Aiglefin à la niçoise.*
▶ *Moules marinières* and *Truite à la vosgienne.*

1 1-kg (2-lb) baby
  haddock
2 tomatoes
150 g (5 oz) onions
butter
1 shallot (optional)
15 ml (1 tablespoon)
  chopped parsley
100 ml (3½ oz) white wine
salt, pepper
*For the sauce:*
  30 ml (2 tablespoons)
  *beurre manié* (p. 87)
  5 ml (1 teaspoon) lemon
  juice
  30 ml (2 tablespoons)
  cream
  chopped parsley for
  garnish

Cut the haddock into slices
about 3 cm (1½ in) thick. Discard the head and tail. Peel,
de-seed and cut the toma-
toes into pieces; peel and
chop the onions very finely.
Butter an ovenproof dish
and put the vegetables and
parsley on to it. Arrange the
slices of fish on top and pour
over the wine. Season well,
cover with tinfoil and bake
in a moderate oven (180°C,
350°F/Gas 4) for 50 min-
utes. When the fish is
cooked, remove it to a serving plate and keep warm.
Transfer the vegetables and
cooking liquor to a saucepan and bring to the boil,
then add the *beurre manié*,
lemon juice and cream. Mix
well and pour over the fish.

## Fried haddock with tomatoes and olives (aiglefin à la niçoise)

*Time* 30 minutes
*Preparation* 30 minutes
*Cooking time* 25 minutes
*Serves* 4

1 baby haddock
flour
90 ml (6 tablespoons)
  olive oil
salt, pepper
75 g (3 oz) anchovy fillets
500 g (1 lb) tomatoes
50 g (2 oz) black olives
2 cloves of garlic, crushed
15 ml (1 tablespoon)
  capers
1 ml (¼ teaspoon) chopped
  tarragon
lemon wedges

Slice the haddock into 6
equal portions, discard the
head and trim off the fins.
Flour the fish slices and fry
them in 60 ml (4 table-
spoons) olive oil over a
moderate heat for about 20
minutes. Season lightly.
Mash two-thirds of the anchovy fillets. Peel the tomatoes and cut them in quarters
and de-seed them. De-stone
the olives. Using 30 ml (2
tablespoons) olive oil, cook
the tomatoes gently for a
few minutes and then add
the olives, mashed ancho-
vies, garlic, capers and tarragon. Season well and
continue cooking for about
5 minutes. Arrange the fish

on a heated plate and surround with the tomato
sauce. Garnish with the remaining anchovies and
wedges of lemon.

## Salt cod with tomatoes and peppers ('la stoccaficada')

*Time* 1½ hours + 3 days
*Preparation* 40 minutes
*Cooking time* 1 hour
*Serves* 8

1 kg (2 lb) stockfish, or
  salt cod
500 g (1 lb) onions
3 green peppers (or,
  preferably, 2 green,
  1 red)
1 kg (2 lb) tomatoes
200 ml (⅓ pint) olive oil
8 cloves garlic, crushed
1 large bouquet garni
4–5 cloves
pepper
1 kg (2 lb) soapy potatoes
8 anchovy fillets
30 ml (2 tablespoons)
  brandy
100 g (4 oz) black olives,
  stoned

Soak the fish for 3 days,
changing the water each
day. Then skin it and remove
any bones, and cut into
pieces, 5 cm (2½ in) wide.
Slice the onions, de-seed
the peppers and cut them
into lengthways strips. Peel
the tomatoes and cut them
into quarters. Heat all but
30 ml (2 tablespoons) of the

▶ Filleting a flat fish.
Remove the head. Cut
down the length of the fish
along the backbone to the
tail (*left*). Gently slice the
fillet away from the bones,
working from the backbone
outwards (*right*).

oil in a large flameproof casserole and fry the onions until they are soft, then add the peppers, tomatoes, garlic, bouquet garni and cloves. Simmer for 12 minutes and then add the fish and 200 ml (⅓ pint) hot water. Season with pepper, bring to the boil and then turn down the heat. Simmer for 30 minutes. At the end of this time, add the potatoes, peeled and cut into thick slices. Push them well down into the casserole and add a little more water if necessary. Cook for a further 25 minutes. Meanwhile, mash the anchovies with the brandy and reserved olive oil. At the end of the cooking, stir in the anchovy purée and olives, and adjust the seasoning. Remove the bouquet garni. Serve in the casserole.

## Mackerel in cream (maquereau fermière)
*Time* 50 minutes
*Preparation* 15 minutes
*Cooking time* 35 minutes
*Serves* 4
4 small mackerel
250 g (8 oz) onions
100 g (4 oz) butter
salt, pepper
100 ml (3½ fl oz) fresh
    cream
grated nutmeg

Wash and clean the mackerel; slash the sides of each 2–3 times. Peel and cut the onions into very thin slices and put them into a well-buttered ovenproof dish. Lay the fish on top and dot with the butter. Season with salt and pepper and bake in a moderate oven (190°C, 375°F/Gas 5) for 35 minutes. Pour the cream over. Add more seasoning if necessary and grate a little nutmeg on top. Return to the oven for a few minutes to heat the cream. *Do not let it boil.*

## Skate with capers (raie aux câpres)
*Time* 45 minutes
*Preparation* 10 minutes
*Cooking time* 10 minutes
*Serves* 4
750 g (1½ lb) skate
court-bouillon (p. 30)
50 g (2 oz) butter
juice of 1 lemon
50 g (2 oz) capers
Soak the skate in cold water for at least 15 minutes. Then poach it in a court-bouillon made with vinegar for about 10 minutes, or until the fish is cooked. Drain. Remove the black skin if necessary. Arrange the pieces of skate on a heated plate and keep warm. Melt the butter and mix in the lemon juice.

Sprinkle the capers over the skate, then pour on the lemon and butter sauce. Serve at once.

## Trout in a red wine sauce (truite à la vosgienne)
*Time* 1 hour 15 minutes
*Preparation* 30 minutes
*Cooking time* 25 minutes
*Serves* 4
600 ml (1 pint) court-
    bouillon made with red
    wine (p. 30)
4 trout*
30 ml (2 tablespoons) flour
75 g (3 oz) butter
salt, pepper
*or delicate-flavoured sea
    fish, such as filleted
    lemon sole, plaice or
    turbot
Make the red-wine court-bouillon. Wash and gut the trout and gently poach them in the court-bouillon for 15 minutes. Then lift them out carefully and keep warm on a serving dish covered with tinfoil. Boil down the stock to reduce it by about half. Work the flour into 50 g (2 oz) of the butter and strain the stock into it. Return to the pan and simmer for 10 minutes. Beat in the remaining butter, check the seasoning and pour the sauce over the trout. Serve very hot, garnished with large croûtons.

◀ Skinning a fish fillet. Lay the fillet skin side down on a flat surface. Starting from the tail end, hold the skin down and with a knife held at an angle of 45° lift off the flesh. Always work towards the head.

# Meat

The French housewife expects to buy all her meat trimmed, boned and even stuffed and rolled ready for her. Veal is more widely available in France than it is in most English-speaking countries. Traditionally, French stews such as estouffades and daubes were not cooked in the oven but in a tightly lidded stewpot over the fire, sometimes with additional coals put into a special hollow in the lid. Nowadays, of course, everybody in France uses an electric or gas cooker rather than an open fire and some people use the oven for long casserole cooking. Standard oven temperatures and timings are given for the recipes in this book.

## Steak with green peppercorns (steak au poivre vert)

*Time* 20 minutes
*Preparation* 5 minutes
*Cooking time* 5–10 minutes
*Serves* 4

500 g (1 lb) frying steak
salt, white pepper
15 g ($\frac{1}{2}$ oz) butter
15 ml (1 tablespoon) oil
100 ml (3$\frac{1}{2}$ fl oz) white wine
15 ml (1 tablespoon) canned green peppercorns, drained
30 ml (2 tablespoons) cream

Trim the steak into 4 equal portions, and beat them with either a meat hammer or the edge of a tea plate to tenderize them. Season with a little salt and freshly

◀ French butchers offer their customers a very wide choice of meats as the display in this Paris *boucherie* proves.

ground white pepper. Heat a frying-pan and add the butter and oil. Fry the steaks over a high heat, turning once, then remove to a warmed plate. *Déglacer* the pan with the wine and add the lightly crushed peppercorns. Stir in the cream away from the heat. Check the seasoning, pour the sauce over the steaks and serve.

**Note** Steak that is about 1 cm ($\frac{1}{2}$ in) thick needs to be fried for 1 minute each side for a rare steak, 2 minutes for a medium steak, and 3 minutes for a well-cooked steak. Grilling times are similar.

## Steak with garlic (steak à l'ail)

*Time* 17 minutes
*Preparation* 7 minutes
*Cooking time* 5–10 minutes
*Serves* 4

500 g (1 lb) frying steak
salt, pepper
2 cloves garlic

15 ml (1 tablespoon) oil
15 g ($\frac{1}{2}$ oz) butter

Divide the steak into 4 portions and trim off any excess fat. Beat with a meat hammer or the edge of a tea-plate if necessary, and sprinkle with a little salt and pepper. Crush the garlic cloves and rub them all over the meat. Heat the oil and butter in a frying-pan and fry the steaks over a high heat, turning once. Serve at once.

**Note** Never turn meat with a fork or knife point when it is frying, since any break in the sealed skin will allow the juices to escape.

## Minced steaks (biftecks des moutiers)

*Time* 1 hour 40 minutes
*Preparation* 1$\frac{1}{2}$ hours
*Cooking time* 10 minutes
*Serves* 6

100 g (4 oz) white bread, without crusts
30 ml (2 tablespoons) milk
1 medium onion

25 g (1 oz) butter
1 beef marrow bone, cut
  into short lengths
600 g (1¼ lb) frying steak,
  minced
2 eggs
salt, pepper
15 ml (1 tablespoon) oil
45 ml (3 tablespoons)
  white wine
60 ml (4 tablespoons)
  stock
tomatoes and parsley for
  garnish

Soak the bread in the milk, and squeeze dry. Chop the onion very finely and gently fry it in a little butter until it is soft but not coloured. Wrap the marrow-bone pieces in tinfoil and poach them in boiling water for 15 minutes. Then scrape out the marrow. Mix the meat, bread, marrow and eggs together very thoroughly, season and leave in a cold place for 1 hour. Form into rissoles and fry in the remaining butter and the oil for about 4 minutes on each side. Remove to a heated plate and *déglacer* the pan with the wine and stock. Check the seasoning and serve the gravy in a separate dish. Garnish the rissoles with grilled tomatoes and fried parsley.

## Beefsteak with red wine sauce (steak à la bordelaise)

*Time* 40 minutes
*Preparation* 30 minutes
*Cooking time* 5–10 minutes
*Serves* 6

6 entrecôte steaks
*Sauce bordelaise:*
  1 marrow bone, cut in
    sections
  200 ml (7 fl oz) red
    wine, preferably
    claret
  30 ml (2 tablespoons)
    finely chopped onions
    or shallots
  10 ml (2 teaspoons)
    tarragon, fresh or dried
  200 ml (7 fl oz) well
    seasoned stock
  25 ml (1½ tablespoons)
    tomato purée
  25 g (1 oz) softened
    butter
  salt and pepper

Trim the steaks to evenly sized portions.

To make the *sauce bordelaise*, either split the marrow bones lengthways, scrape out the marrow and poach it in boiling salted water for 3 minutes, *or* wrap each section of the bone in tinfoil and cook in boiling water for 15 minutes, then remove the marrow and keep warm. Put the red wine, chopped onions or shallots and tarragon in an enamel or non-stick saucepan. Boil until the liquid is reduced by half. Add the stock and tomato purée and simmer for 12 minutes. Strain through a fine sieve and keep warm.

Spread a little butter on each steak and cook under a very hot grill, turning once. Season each side after it is cooked. The length of cooking will depend on the thickness of the steak.

To serve, mix the marrow with the sauce, pour over the steaks and serve very hot.

## Beef in red wine (boeuf bourguignonne)

*Time* 2 hours 15 minutes
*Preparation* 10 minutes
*Cooking time* 2 hours
*Serves* 4

750 g (1½ lb) braising
  steak
20 g (¾ oz) lard
15 ml (1 tablespoon) flour
200 ml (7 fl oz) stock
200 ml (7 fl oz) red wine,
  preferably Burgundy
1 onion stuck with 2
  cloves
bouquet garni with garlic
salt, pepper

◀ *Left* Marmite for making stocks and *pot-au-feu*. The shape minimizes evaporation. *Right Cocotte* made of enamelled cast iron, used either on the hob or in the oven.

◀ To *déglacer* a pan for a sauce, pour wine or stock into a pan in which the meat has been fried. Stir well over a high heat to incorporate all the caramelized meat juices into the sauce.

Cut the meat into 5-cm (2-in) cubes. Brown in the lard, then sprinkle the flour over and cook for a minute more. Add the stock, wine, onion and bouquet garni. Season well and cook, tightly covered, for 2 hours in a slow oven (160°C, 325°F/Gas 3). Check the seasoning and remove onion and bouquet garni before serving.

### Goulash with beer (goulache à la bière)
*Time* 2 hours 20 minutes
*Preparation* 20 minutes
*Cooking time* 2 hours
*Serves* 4
750 g (1½ lb) braising beef
150 g (5 oz) onions
15 ml (1 tablespoon) lard
15 ml (1 tablespoon) flour
2·5 ml (½ teaspoon) paprika
bouquet garni
2 cloves garlic
30 ml (2 tablespoons) tomato purée *or* 350 g (12 oz) tomatoes
300 ml (½ pint) beer
salt, pepper
10 ml (2 teaspoons) sugar

Remove all fat from the meat and cut into 4–8 serving portions. Fry them with the sliced onions in the lard. Sprinkle the flour on top and turn until well browned. Add the paprika, bouquet garni, crushed garlic and tomato purée or tomatoes, peeled and de-seeded, and the beer. Season, add the sugar and cook, covered, either over a gentle heat for 2 hours or in a moderate oven (180°C, 350°F/Gas 4) for 1¾ hours. Adjust the seasoning and remove the bouquet garni before serving.

### Pot au feu (pot-au-feu du languedoc)
*Time* 3 hours 40 minutes
*Preparation* 40 minutes
*Cooking time* 3 hours
*Serves* 8–10
750 g (1½ lb) silverside
750 g (1½ lb) forerib
500 g (1 lb) knuckle of veal, cut into short lengths
400 g (12 oz) unsmoked bacon, in one piece
1 marrow bone

300 g (10 oz) leeks
300 g (10 oz) carrots
300 g (10 oz) white turnips
3 litres (5¼ pints) water
salt
3 cloves garlic
1 stick celery
10 peppercorns
1 large onion stuck with 3 cloves
bouquet garni
Trim off any excess fat from the meat. Remove any fragments of bone from the veal. Blanch the bacon in boiling water for 15 minutes. Tie the marrow bone in a piece of cloth so that the marrow cannot escape during cooking. Wash the leeks thoroughly and tie them together to prevent them falling apart during cooking. Peel the carrots and turnips.
Put the water on to boil in a very large saucepan or casserole with 15 ml (1 tablespoon) salt. When the water is boiling, put in the silverside, forerib and bacon with the garlic, celery, peppercorns, onion, bouquet garni and marrow bone.

▲ Marinading beef for *boeuf en daube*.

## Marinades

Marinades are used to tenderize and improve the flavour of meat, particularly game, or to give butchers' meat a slightly gamey flavour. French marinades are all based on vinegar or wine, with salt, herbs, spices and often vegetables added. Some marinades are cooked before use — normally those for large pieces of meat requiring long soaking. Cooking the marinade strengthens the effect of the salt and herbs. Uncooked marinades are usually for meats that require flavouring rather than tenderizing, and will soak for a shorter time. No marinade should ever touch metal; china or Pyrex bowls are the most suitable receptacles and a wooden spoon should be used for turning or basting the meat. The length of time necessary for marinating varies from one to six days, more in cold weather than in warm. The marinade is used in the dish itself, too, either for cooking the meat in or for the accompanying sauce, because of the close affinity marinating creates between the meat and liquid.

Simmer for 1½ hours over a low heat, skimming from time to time. Then add the carrots, turnips, leeks and knuckle of veal and cook for another 1½ hours. Check the seasoning during this period.

To serve, take out the meat, remove the cloth from the marrow bone and carve the meats. Keep warm on a heated plate. Remove and drain the vegetables and un-tie the leeks. Arrange the vegetables around the meat. When the soup has cooled a little, skim off the fat, then strain through a fine *wet* cloth. Check the seasoning and serve the soup in a separate tureen. Pickles, gherkins, mustard and bread are the traditional accom-paniments to this dish.

## Casserole of beef with red wine (boeuf en daube)

*Time* 4½ hours + overnight
*Preparation* 15 + 20 minutes
*Cooking time* 4 hours
*Serves* 6

1 kg (2 lb) chuck steak
*Marinade:*
    100 g (4 oz) onion, sliced
    30 ml (2 tablespoons) oil
2 cloves garlic
200 ml (7 fl oz) red wine
1 clove
bouquet garni
salt, pepper
150 g (5 oz) fat bacon, in one piece

▶ Renoir's painting 'Luncheon of the Boating Party' forms a beautiful backdrop for this typical French family meal: *moules marinières, poulet à l'ail* and apricot and strawberry tarts.

40

100 g (4 oz) onion,
sliced
300 ml ($\frac{1}{2}$ pint) boiling
stock
salt, pepper

Cut the meat into pieces about 6 x 2 cm (3 x 1 in). Soak in the marinade overnight (see photograph on p. 40). The next day simmer the bacon in water for 15 minutes and then cut into pieces. Put the bacon in the bottom of a casserole and lay the sliced onion on top. Then pack the meat in firmly, and add all the marinade and enough boiling stock almost to cover the meat. Season and cover the casserole tightly. Cook for 4 hours in a slow oven (160°C, 325°F/Gas 4). Remove the bouquet garni before serving.

## Beef set in jelly (boeuf en gelée)

*Time* 2–3 days
*Preparation* 1 hour 15 minutes
*Cooking time* 3 hours
*Serves* 6–8

1·5 kg (3 lb) topside
50 g (2 oz) strips of pork
fat or unsmoked bacon
for larding
*Marinade:*
1 onion
1 carrot
400 ml ($\frac{3}{4}$ pint) red wine
salt, pepper
1 large bouquet garni
1 clove
25 g (1 oz) butter
1 litre (1$\frac{1}{2}$ pints) stock
3 pig's trotters

Lard the beef with the strips of pork fat and marinate for 12 hours, turning the meat from time to time. Drain,

wipe dry, then fry in the butter until brown on all sides. Place in a large casserole and add the marinade, stock and pig's trotters. Bring to the boil, lower the heat and skim for about 10 minutes. Cover the casserole and place in a low oven (150°C, 300°F/Gas 2) for 3 hours.

Remove the beef and fit it tightly into a bowl that will give it a firm, round shape, cover and press. Leave to get cold. Strain the stock, which should have reduced to about 600 ml (1 pint), through a fine cloth. Check the seasoning and leave to cool. When the stock has set into jelly, carefully scrape off the surface fat. Warm the jelly to running point and pour a little into the bottom of a mould to coat it. When that has set, put the meat, now set in a round, into the mould and pour the remaining jelly over it. Leave in the refrigerator for about 6 hours to set firmly. Unmould before serving.

## Braised veal with vegetables (sauté de veau andalou)

*Time* 1 hour
*Preparation* 30 minutes
*Cooking time* 30 minutes
*Serves* 4

500 g (1 lb) veal, cut from
the leg but with no bone
250 g (8 oz) green peppers
3 tomatoes
200 g (6 oz) chopped
onion
200 g (6 oz) button
mushrooms
25 g (1 oz) butter

30 ml (2 tablespoons) oil
20 ml (4 teaspoons)
tomato ketchup
2 cloves garlic
salt, pepper

Cut the veal into cubes. Deseed the peppers and cut into pieces. Skin the tomatoes and cut into quarters. Chop the onion and wipe the mushrooms but leave whole. Fry the veal in the butter and oil until well browned. Remove to a plate. Fry the onion in the same fat. After a few minutes add the peppers, tomatoes and mushrooms and continue cooking for another 3–4 minutes. Return the veal to the pan and add the tomato ketchup, crushed garlic and seasoning. Cover the pan and continue cooking over a low heat for 30 minutes. Check the seasoning before serving.

## Casserole of veal (veal Marengo)

*Time* 1 hour 50 minutes
*Preparation* 15 minutes
*Cooking time* 1$\frac{1}{2}$ hours
*Serves* 6

1 kg (2 lb) stewing veal
15 ml (1 tablespoon) olive
oil
25 g (1 oz) butter
salt, pepper
1 large onion
1 clove garlic
200 ml (7 fl oz) stock
100 ml (3$\frac{1}{2}$ fl oz) white
wine
bouquet garni
30 ml (2 tablespoons)
tomato purée
15 ml (1 tablespoon)
*beurre manié* (p. 87)

Cut the meat into pieces and fry it in the oil and butter.

Season and add the onion and garlic, both finely chopped. Cook for a few moments, then add the stock, wine, bouquet garni and tomato purée. Bring back to the boil, then *either* cover and cook gently for 1½ hours *or* place in a moderate oven (180 C, 350°F/Gas 4) for the same time. Just before serving, remove the bouquet garni and mix the *beurre manié* in well.

## Roast lamb with juniper berries
## (gigot au genièvre)
*Time* 2 days
*Preparation* 10 minutes
*Cooking time* 1 hour 40
    minutes
*Serves* 6
1½-kg (3-lb) leg of lamb
30 juniper berries
15 ml (1 tablespoon) oil
salt, pepper
200 ml (7 fl oz) chicken
    stock
Wipe the lamb and make small incisions with a knife all over the outside skin. Push 20 crushed juniper berries into the cuts and

▶ A cast iron *grille*, which is used over a hot plate or gas ring, should always be heated before the food is put on it. Meat should not be salted before it is grilled because the salt draws the moisture from the meat to the surface and so hinders the caramelizing process that gives grilled meat its succulent skin. However, when grilling lamb chops with herbs this rule must be broken.

leave for 2 days in a cool place. Meanwhile, gently heat the oil with 10 juniper berries, then leave to infuse for 12 hours. Rub the meat with a little salt and pepper and then paint it all over with the flavoured oil. Roast the meat on a rack in a roasting tin, basting from time to time, in a moderate oven (190°C, 375°F/Gas 5) for 1 hour 40 minutes (25 minutes per 500 g/1 lb plus 25 minutes). Make the gravy by pouring off the fat and boiling the meat juices in the roasting tin with the chicken stock. Check the seasoning and serve in a separate gravy dish.
**Note** The French prefer to eat roast lamb underdone. Their cooking-time allowance is only 15 minutes per 500 g (1 lb). If you wish to serve lamb in the authentic French style, decrease the cooking time accordingly.

## Braised shoulder of lamb
## (épaule d'agneau au romarin)
*Time* 2 hours 55 minutes

*Preparation* 45 minutes
*Cooking time* 2 hours 35
    minutes
*Serves* 6
1·25-kg (2½-lb) shoulder
    of lamb
1 kg (2 lb) potatoes
350 g (12 oz) onions
2 cloves garlic
250 g (8 oz) tomatoes
300 ml (½ pint) milk
salt, pepper
6 branches rosemary
50 g (2 oz) butter
oil
Ask the butcher to bone the joint. Peel the potatoes, onions and garlic and skin the tomatoes. Cut all into thin slices and arrange them in a deep, well-buttered casserole. Pour over the milk, add 2·5 ml (½ teaspoon) salt and 1 ml (¼ teaspoon) pepper and cook in a moderate oven (190°C, 375°F/Gas 5) for 35 minutes. Meanwhile, remove the leaves from two branches of rosemary and chop finely. Beat the chopped rosemary into the butter and season generously. Spread the herb butter over the inside of the meat,

43

roll up and tie securely. Paint the outside of the roll with oil and tuck the remaining rosemary branches under the string around the meat. Put the joint on top of the vegetables and cook for a further 2 hours in the oven (allowing 30 minutes per 500 g/1 lb plus 30 minutes). Serve in the casserole.

### Grilled lamb chops with thyme
### (agneau grillé au thym)
*Time* 30 minutes
*Preparation* 15 minutes
*Cooking time* 16 minutes
*Serves* 4
4 small leg chops
4 branches thyme *or* 2·5 ml (½ teaspoon) dried thyme
30 ml (2 tablespoons) oil
salt, pepper
1 clove garlic
15 g (½ oz) butter

Trim the chops. Crumble the thyme and put it in the oil to draw out the flavour. Season the chops lightly and rub them over with the garlic. Then paint them with the thyme and oil and leave on one side for 10 minutes. Heat a grill pan (see p. 43) to very hot and cook the chops for about 8 minutes on each side. Serve at once with a little butter on each chop.

### Pork chops with gherkins
### (échine de porc Célestine)
*Time* 25 minutes
*Preparation* 5 minutes
*Cooking time* 20 minutes
*Serves* 4
4 pork chops
15 g (½ oz) butter
15 ml (1 tablespoon) oil
1 clove garlic
salt, pepper
45 ml (3 tablespoons) white wine
5 ml (1 teaspoon) French mustard
3 gherkins, chopped
15 ml (1 tablespoon) chopped parsley
100 ml (3½ fl oz) cream

Fry the pork chops in the butter and oil, add the garlic, crushed, towards the end of the cooking, together with the salt and pepper. Put the meat on a heated plate and keep warm. *Déglacer* the pan with the wine, add the mustard and mix well. Then add the gherkins, the parsley and cream. Pour the sauce over the chops and serve.

### Pork chops with apples and oranges
### (côtes de porc bichette)
*Time* 35 minutes
*Preparation* 15 minutes
*Cooking time* 20 minutes
*Serves* 4
4 evenly sized pork chops
2 cloves
pinch sea salt
1 ml (¼ teaspoon) freshly ground black pepper
pinch grated nutmeg
3 Golden Delicious apples
50 g (2 oz) butter
2 oranges

Trim the pork chops. Crush the cloves and mix them with the salt, black pepper and grated nutmeg. Rub the chops with this mixture.

◄ *Côtes de porc bichette.*
► *Agneau grillé au thym* with *tomates farcies au maigre* and *pommes de terre estivales.*

Peel, core and slice the apples, and gently poach them in half the butter. Squeeze 1 orange and cut the other into very thin slices. Fry the chops on both sides in the remaining butter. Arrange on a heated plate and surround with the apples. Cook the orange slices gently in the remaining meat juices and arrange them on the plate. Finally, *déglacer* the pan with the orange juice and pour the sauce over the chops. Serve very hot.

## Casserole of pork and beans (cassoulet de Carcassonne)
*Time* at least 2 days
*Preparation* 1 hour
*Final cooking time* 1 hour
*Serves* 8
1 pig's trotter
500 g (1 lb) pork hock
1 large bouquet garni
1 onion stuck with 5 cloves
1·5 litres (2½ pints) water
500 g (1 lb) dry haricot
  beans
5 ml (1 teaspoon) salt
2·5 ml (½ teaspoon)
  freshly ground black
  pepper
500 g (1 lb) belly of pork,
  boned
8 cloves garlic
2 large onions, chopped
500 g (1 lb) Cumberland
  *or* thick pork sausages
2 pieces *confit d'oie, or*
  1 wing and drumstick of
  a roast goose, *or* pieces
  of any roast game such
  as rabbit, hare or game
  bird
breadcrumbs (optional)

Cook the trotter and hock with the bouquet garni and onion stuck with cloves in the water for 2 hours. Skim when it first boils, then lower the heat and simmer. When cooked, leave to cool in the stock. Soak the haricot beans in cold water overnight. The next day, remove the bones from the trotter and hock, cut the skin from the hock into squares and put it with the meat and jelly. Strain the stock and reserve.

Rinse the beans and put them on to cook in cold water. Immediately the water boils, strain the beans and throw away the water. Return the beans to the saucepan with the meat, jelly, skin, salt, pepper and enough of the stock to cover the beans. (Add water if there is not enough stock.) Simmer for 2 hours.

Meanwhile, skin the pork belly and cut the meat and fat into 2-cm (1-in) cubes. Put them into a frying-pan, without additional fat, and cook over a gentle heat until the fat runs. Then add the crushed garlic and chopped onions and cook for about 20 minutes. Meanwhile, grill the sausages until they are well cooked—about 20 minutes. Mix the belly of pork, onions and garlic into the beans and continue cooking for another 15 minutes. Cut the sausages and *confit d'oie*, goose or game into 4-cm (2-in) pieces. Test the beans for seasoning, then put about half in a large earthenware casserole. Lay the goose pieces on top and

cover with the rest of the beans. Finish with a layer of the sausages. Cook, without a lid, in a moderate oven (180°C, 350°F/Gas 4) for 20 minutes. Then take out and leave to cool overnight.

The next day, re-heat for at least 1 hour, with the casserole uncovered. To make a crisper crust, sprinkle with breadcrumbs and splash with a little water before the final cooking.

## Braised pork with leeks (sauté de porc aux poireaux)
*Time* 1 hour 25 minutes
*Preparation* 20 minutes
*Cooking time* 1 hour
*Serves* 4
This dish, from Alsace-Lorraine, is more typically German than French.
500 g (1 lb) pork shoulder,
  boned
4 leeks
750 g (1½ lb) potatoes
2 onions
30 ml (2 tablespoons) oil
1 litre (1¾ pints) well-
  seasoned stock
salt, pepper
Cut the meat into cubes. Wash and cut the leeks into rings. Peel and cut the potatoes into small pieces. Chop the onions. Heat the oil in a casserole and fry the pork and onions, then add the leeks and cook gently until they are soft. Pour over the stock, season, cover and leave to cook for 30 minutes. Add the potatoes and cook for a further 30 minutes. Check the seasoning and serve very hot.

## Ham with sage in a pastry case (jambon en croûte à la sauge)

*Time* 24 hours
*Preparation* 1 hour
*Final cooking time* 50 minutes
*Serves* 6

2 kg (4 lb) middle-cut gammon
4 carrots, sliced
1 stick celery
1 bay leaf
6 sprigs parsley
1 bunch fresh sage *or* 60 ml (4 tablespoons) dried sage
200 ml (7 fl oz) dry white wine
750 g (1½ lb) puff pastry
1 egg yolk
*Sauce:*
1 tomato
25 g (1 oz) mushrooms
15 g (½ oz) butter
15 ml (1 tablespoon) flour
salt, pepper
30 ml (2 tablespoons) cream

Soak the ham for 12 hours in cold water. Then place in a large saucepan with the carrots, celery, bay leaf, parsley and about one-third of the sage, cover with water and bring to the boil. Turn down the heat and simmer for 80 minutes (20 minutes per 500 g/1 lb). Leave to cool in the stock.

When cold, cut off the skin and all but a thin layer of the surrounding fat. Strain and reserve the stock for the sauce. Rub the ham all over with more sage and put it in an ovenproof dish with the wine and remaining sage. Bake in a moderate oven (180°C, 350°F/Gas 4) for 35 minutes, basting frequently. Remove to a clean plate and allow to cool. Rinse off any stray pieces of sage, pat dry and carve into slices (picture 1).

Roll the pastry out to ½ cm (¼ in) thick and cut into 1 strip long enough and wide enough to encase the ham, and into 2 equal rounds for the top and bottom of the pastry case. Take care the rounds are big enough to allow the ham slices to be lifted out easily when the top is removed. Reassemble the ham and wrap it in the pastry (picture 2). Overlap the joints and seal firmly with water (picture 3). Glaze with egg yolk and bake in a hot oven (220°C, 425°F/ Gas 7) for 50 minutes. Cover with greaseproof paper after 25 minutes to stop it getting too brown.

For the sauce, cook the tomato and mushrooms in 400 ml (¾ pint) of the reserved stock for 15 minutes, then strain. Make a brown roux with the butter and flour, season and add the prepared stock. Bring to the boil and simmer for 10 minutes, stirring occasionally. Check the seasoning and stir in the cream just before serving.

## Rabbit with olives (lapin aux olives)

*Time* 1 hour 35 minutes
*Preparation* 10 minutes
*Cooking time* 1 hour 20 minutes
*Serves* 4

300 g (10 oz) onions
750 g (1½ lb) rabbit joints

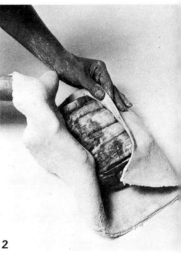

▼ *Jambon en croute* served with *brioches en pommes de terre* and *choux de Bruxelles*.

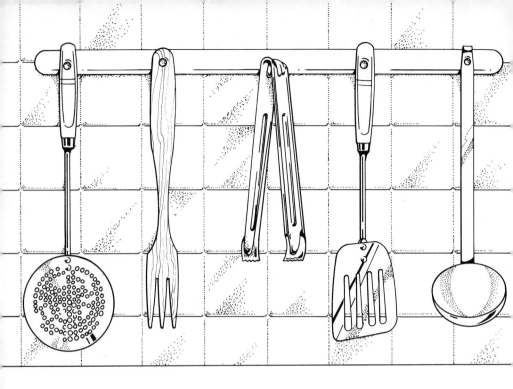

45 ml (3 tablespoons) olive oil
10 ml (2 teaspoons) flour
100 ml (3½ fl oz) white wine
salt, pepper
rosemary
50 g (2 oz) black olives
chopped parsley for garnish

Slice the onions thinly. Heat the oil in a frying-pan and fry the rabbit gently. When it has changed colour add the onions and flour. Stir for a moment to mix well and then moisten with the wine. Add salt, pepper and a little rosemary, cover and cook gently for 50 minutes. Then add the olives and cook for another 30 minutes. Adjust the seasoning and serve very hot sprinkled with parsley.

## Auvergne rabbit casserole (lapin à l'auvergnate)

*Time* 2¼ hours
*Preparation* 30 minutes
*Cooking time* 1½ hours
*Serves* 4

600 g (1¼ lb) hearted cabbage
salt
100 g (4 oz) bacon, in one piece
4 thin pork sausages
25 g (1 oz) butter
30 ml (2 tablespoons) oil
750 g (1½ lb) rabbit joints
1 big bouquet garni
6 small onions
pepper

Wash and cut the cabbage into quarters. Plunge into salted, boiling water, cook for 12 minutes, then remove and drain. Simmer the bacon in boiling water for 15 minutes, then drain and cut into dice. Grill or fry the sausages until they are browned all over. In a flameproof casserole melt the butter and oil and fry the bacon dice, then remove and fry the rabbit until lightly browned on all sides. Add the bouquet garni, cabbage, onions, peeled but whole, bacon dice and the sausages. Season with pepper only. Cover and cook very gently for 1½ hours. Before serving, remove the bouquet garni and check the seasoning.

▶ Choose a kitchen knife that feels right for your hand and make sure it is sharpened very frequently.

50

## Roast venison (selle de chevreuil à la sauce poivrade)

*Time* 27 hours
*Preparation* 15 minutes + 50 minutes
*Cooking time* 1 hour 40 minutes
*Serves* 8

1·5–2 kg (3–4 lb) saddle of venison
*Marinade:*
  1 bottle red wine (claret or Burgundy)
  10 juniper berries
  10 peppercorns
  1 large bouquet garni
  50 g (2 oz) carrots, sliced
  50 g (2 oz) sliced onion
*Sauce:*
  scraps of venison, trimmed from the joint
  1 carrot, sliced
  1 onion, sliced
  25 g (1 oz) lard
  30 ml (2 tablespoons) flour
  1¾ litres (3 pints) stock

200 ml (7 fl oz) red wine, taken from the marinade
bouquet garni
1 small slice chilli
salt, pepper
15 ml (1 tablespoon) redcurrant jelly
250 g (8 oz) strips of back pork fat or fat bacon for larding.
500 g (1 lb) pears
15 ml (1 tablespoon) sugar
5 ml (1 teaspoon) cinnamon

Trim the joint and marinate for 24 hours, turning frequently. Meanwhile, make the sauce by browning the venison trimmings and the vegetables in the lard. Remove, then fry the flour in the remaining fat until it is just brown. Add more lard if necessary. Return the meat scraps and vegetables, add the stock, red wine and bouquet garni and bring to the boil. Turn down the heat,

skim carefully and leave to simmer for 4 hours.

Strain the stock, return to a clean pan and simmer for another 5 minutes with the chilli. Then *remove the chilli.* Check the seasoning of the sauce — it should taste pleasantly peppery — and leave on one side in a clean bowl.

Before roasting the venison, lard it with short strips of pork fat, leaving about 3 cm (1½ in) between each strip. Cover the top of the joint with pieces of pork fat and wrap the whole in tinfoil. Stand the joint, top side up, in a roasting tin and cook in a moderate oven (190°C, 375°F/Gas 5) for 25 minutes per 500 g (1 lb).

Before serving, re-heat the sauce and stir in the redcurrant jelly. Serve the sauce in a separate dish. Garnish the joint with pears stewed with sugar and cinnamon.

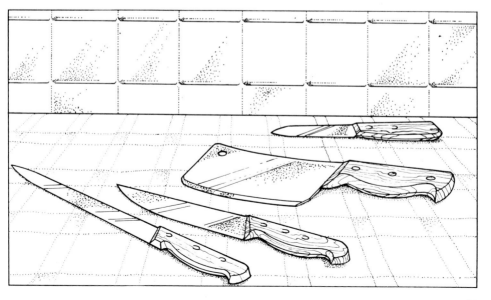

51

# Poultry

A wide choice of fresh poultry is available to the French housewife, including geese, ducks, turkeys, guinea fowl, pigeons and various sorts of chicken. Frozen chickens are not common, but can be found in the hypermarkets. Until production methods adopted during the last twenty years made chickens less expensive, chicken was considered special in France—as it was in most countries. Nowadays, however, chicken is a good standby for everyday family meals.

## Chicken with tomatoes and peppers (poulet basque)
*Time* 1¼ hours
*Preparation* 25 minutes
*Cooking time* 45 minutes
*Serves* 4–6
1·5 kg (3 lb) chicken
4 cloves garlic
45 ml (3 tablespoons) olive oil
250 g (8 oz) onions
100 g (4 oz) mushrooms
500 g (1 lb) tomatoes
500 g (1 lb) peppers
bunch of parsley
salt, pepper

Joint the chicken and brown it with the garlic in two-thirds of the olive oil, turning frequently so that it browns evenly and does not stick. Chop the onions and mushrooms finely. Peel, quarter and de-seed the tomatoes. De-seed the peppers and cut into thin slices. In a separate pan cook all the vegetables in the remaining olive oil. When soft, add to the chicken with the parsley, salt and pepper. Cover and leave to cook for ¾ hour over a low heat. Remove the bunch of parsley before serving.

## Chicken and bacon (poulet de ma marraine)
*Time* 1 hour 20 minutes
*Preparation* 15 minutes
*Cooking time* 1 hour
*Serves* 4
1·5-kg (3-lb) chicken
8 thin rashers of bacon
2 medium onions
butter
1 clove garlic, crushed
3 tomatoes
bouquet garni
salt, pepper
15 ml (1 tablespoon) oil

Joint the chicken and wrap a rasher of bacon round each joint. Cut the onions into rings and place in the bottom of a well-buttered oven-proof dish with the crushed garlic. Lay the chicken joints on the onions. Peel, quarter and de-seed the tomatoes. Add to the dish with the bouquet garni. Season well and sprinkle with the oil. Cover with tinfoil and cook for 1 hour in a moderate oven (190°C, 375°F/Gas 5). Remove the bouquet garni and serve in the ovenproof dish.

## Chicken with tarragon (poulet nantais)
*Time* 1½ hours
*Preparation* 25 minutes
*Cooking time* 55 minutes
*Serves* 4
1·25-kg (2½-lb) chicken
4 shallots *or* 50 g (2 oz) onion
bunch of fresh tarragon *or* 5 ml (1 teaspoon) dry tarragon
25 g (1 oz) butter
45 ml (3 tablespoons) brandy
150 ml (¼ pint) white wine
150 ml (¼ pint) water
salt, pepper
2 egg yolks
100 ml (3½ fl oz) cream

Cut the chicken into joints.

**1**

Chop the shallots or onion finely. If using the fresh herb, strip the tarragon leaves from the stalks and chop them and tie the stalks into a bunch like a bouquet garni. Brown the chicken in the butter. When thoroughly browned, pour in the brandy and light it. Then remove the chicken and fry the shallots or onion until transparent. Return the chicken with the tarragon stalks or half the dried tarragon and add the white wine, water, salt and pepper. Cover the pan and leave to cook for 50 minutes on a low heat.

Then put the chicken on a warm plate and strain the cooking liquor. Return it to a clean saucepan and boil for 2 minutes to reduce it. Beat the eggs and cream together. Remove the saucepan from the heat, add a little of the liquid to the cream and eggs and then pour the mixture into the saucepan. Return it to a very low heat, stirring all the time; *do not let it boil*. Add the chopped tarragon (or the rest of the dried tarragon), check the season- ing, pour over the chicken joints and serve.

**2**

### Jointing a chicken
Pull the legs away from the body and cut through the ball joint at the hip. Cut through the shoulder joint at the bottom of the breast to remove the wings. Cut off the scaly part at the bottom of each leg and cut the flight from each wing (**1**).

Cut through the ribs to remove the breast section from the backbone (**2**).

Divide the breast in two by cutting through the bone along the line of the breast bone (**3**).

The chicken joints can be further divided by cutting the legs in half at the joint (**4**). The breast can be entirely deboned if preferred.

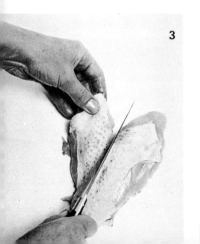

**3**

**4**

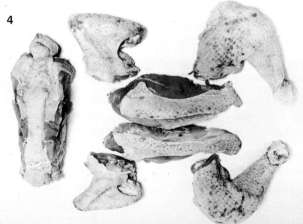

## Fried chicken with orange and lemon (poulet sudiste)

*Time* 1 hour
*Preparation* 25 minutes
*Cooking time* 35 minutes
*Serves* 4

1½-kg (3-lb) chicken
45 ml (3 tablespoons) flour
  seasoned with:
  5 ml (1 teaspoon) grated
    nutmeg
  5 ml (1 teaspoon) salt
  1 ml ($\frac{1}{4}$ teaspoon)
    cayenne
  1 ml ($\frac{1}{4}$ teaspoon)
    freshly ground black
    pepper
  grated rind of 1 orange
  grated rind of 1 lemon
100 g (4 oz) lard
100 g (4 oz) butter
2 cloves

Cut the chicken into joints and roll in the seasoned flour. Fry the chicken in the lard and butter over a gentle heat for 20 minutes. Turn from time to time to brown evenly. Then transfer to an ovenproof dish with a few spoonfuls of the cooking juices and the cloves. Cover and cook for a further 15 minutes in a moderate oven (180°C, 350°F/Gas 4). Serve in the ovenproof dish.

## Chicken casserole with red wine (coq au vin)

*Time* 1½ hours
*Preparation* 35 minutes
*Cooking time* 45 minutes
*Serves* 4

1½-kg (3-lb) chicken
100 g (4 oz) unsmoked
  bacon, in one piece
100 g (4 oz) carrots
15 small onions *or* 125 g
  (5 oz) chopped onion

2 tomatoes
100 g (4 oz) mushrooms
15 ml (1 tablespoon) oil
25 g (1 oz) butter
30 ml (2 tablespoons)
  brandy
750 ml (1¼ pints) red wine,
  preferably Beaujolais
bouquet garni
salt, pepper
30 ml (2 tablespoons)
  *beurre manié*
garlic croûtons

Joint the chicken. Simmer the bacon in boiling water for 15 minutes and then cut into small cubes. Slice the carrots into rounds. Peel the onions and leave them whole. Quarter and de-seed the tomatoes. Wipe and remove the stalks of the mushrooms. In a large casserole gently fry the carrots, onions and bacon in the oil and butter for a few minutes. Remove to a plate. Brown the chicken on all sides in the same fat, then pour in the

▲ When frying croûtons, take care that the fat does not get too hot or they will burn.

brandy. Light it and when it has finished burning put the chicken on the plate with the vegetables. Pour the wine into the casserole, add the bouquet garni and *boil hard* for 5 minutes. Return the chicken, vegetables and bacon to the casserole, add the mushrooms and tomatoes and season well. Cover closely and cook in a moderate oven (180°C, 350°F/Gas 4) for 40 minutes. Before serving, remove the bouquet garni, add the *beurre manié* and stir carefully until dissolved.

Check the seasoning. Serve in the casserole. Garnish with croûtons of fried bread rubbed with garlic.

◀ *Poulet nantais.*

▶ *Oie aux pruneaux* with *pommes galentier* and *tomates provençales.*

gravy. Check the seasoning, add the lemon juice and then return to the saucepan and carefully re-heat. *Do not boil.* Pour some of the sauce over the chicken and serve the rest in a sauce bowl.

### Chicken-in-the-pot (poule à la béarnaise)
*Time* 4 hours 45 minutes
*Preparation* 45 minutes
*Cooking time* 4 hours
*Serves* 6
2-kg (4-lb) boiling fowl
75 g (3 oz) lean minced
   pork *or* sausage meat
25 g (1 oz) crustless bread
milk
1 clove garlic
15 ml (1 tablespoon)
   chopped parsley
1 egg
salt, pepper
3 carrots
1 onion
1 stalk celery
2 turnips
1 leek
1 large bouquet garni
Mince the liver and heart of the chicken with the pork. Soak the bread in the milk, then squeeze dry. Mix the minced meat with the bread, crushed garlic and parsley. Bind with the beaten egg and season with salt and pepper. Remove any loose fat from the inside of the chicken and stuff it with this mixture. Sew the vent up very tightly. Truss the chicken, making sure that both ends are closed firmly.

### Chicken casserole with white wine (poulet Mme Maigret)
*Time* 1 hour 20 minutes
*Preparation* 35 minutes
*Cooking time* 40 minutes
*Serves* 4
1½-kg (3-lb) chicken
2 carrots
4 shallots *or* 1 onion
25 g (1 oz) butter
15 ml (1 tablespoon) oil
2 cloves garlic, crushed
10 ml (2 teaspoons) flour
45 ml (3 tablespoons)
   brandy
150 ml (¼ pint) white
   wine, preferably Riesling
150 ml (¼ pint) stock
bouquet garni
pinch grated nutmeg
salt, pepper
1 egg yolk
45 ml (3 tablespoons)
   cream
15 ml (1 tablespoon)
   lemon juice

Cut the chicken into joints. Cut the carrots and shallots or onion into very small pieces. In a large casserole, fry the chicken pieces in the butter and oil until well browned. Put aside and fry the vegetables and garlic. After a few minutes, return the chicken to the pan and sprinkle the flour over. Mix in well, then pour in the brandy and light it. When it has finished burning, add the wine and stock and turn up the heat. Stir well to mix in all the scraps from the bottom of the pan. Add the bouquet garni, nutmeg and seasoning. Cover and leave to simmer on a low heat for 40 minutes. When the chicken is cooked, remove to a heated serving dish and keep warm. Strain the gravy. Mix the egg yolk and cream in a bowl and slowly add the

Put the chicken into a large saucepan with all the vegetables, washed and roughly chopped, the bouquet garni, salt and pepper. Cover completely with cold water. Bring to the boil, turn down the heat and skim the surface for a few minutes. Cover and leave to cook on a very low heat for 4 hours. Then lift out the chicken and untie the string. Serve on a heated plate with a *sauce poulette* (p. 83). Strain the soup, discarding the vegetables, and either skim off the fat and serve the stock as a soup before the chicken, or reserve for another occasion.

## Roast chicken with garlic
## (poulet à l'ail)

*Time* 1½ hours
*Preparation* 10 minutes
*Cooking time* 1 hour 20 minutes
*Serves* 4–5
6 cloves garlic
1·5-kg (3-lb) chicken
1 branch rosemary
3 branches thyme
25 g (1 oz) butter
salt, pepper
150 ml (¼ pint) chicken stock

Peel the garlic and place inside the chicken. Truss ready for roasting. Chop the rosemary and thyme very finely and mash them into the softened butter with salt and pepper. Make small incisions in the skin over the breast and legs of the chicken and slide some of the seasoned butter between the skin and flesh. Spread the remaining butter all over the outside of the chicken and put it on a rack in a roasting tin in a hot oven (190°C, 375°F/Gas 5) and cook for 1 hour 20 minutes, basting from time to time. Untie and serve on a hot plate. To make the gravy, pour off almost all the fat and *déglacer* the roasting tin with the chicken stock. Boil for a few moments, check the seasoning and serve in a gravy boat.

## Roast chicken with cream cheese and port
## (poulet farci au porto)

*Time* 2 hours 10 minutes
*Preparation* 40 minutes
*Cooking time* 1½ hours
*Serves* 6–8
2-kg (4-lb) roasting chicken
salt

freshly milled white pepper
500 g (1 lb) mushrooms
100 g (4 oz) butter
2 chicken livers
100 g (4 oz) almonds
50 g (2 oz) bread without crusts
a little milk
10 ml (2 teaspoons) chopped parsley
1 clove garlic, crushed
2 portions *Petit Suisse* or 40 g (1½ oz) cream cheese
2 eggs, beaten
200 ml (7 fl oz) port
100 ml (3½ fl oz) cream
Wipe the chicken and season the inside generously. Wash and trim the mushrooms. Chop half of them finely and cook in a little butter. Mince the chicken livers. De-skin and roughly chop the almonds. Soak the bread in a little milk and squeeze dry. In a bowl mix the cooked mushrooms with the chicken livers, bread, almonds, parsley, garlic and cream cheese. Add the beaten eggs and 60 ml (4 tablespoons) port. Mix thoroughly. Stuff the chicken with this mixture and truss it firmly to ensure that none of the stuffing escapes during the cooking. Spread a little butter, salt and pepper over the outside of the bird. Cook, in an oiled roasting tin, in a moderately hot oven (190°C, 375°F/Gas 5) for 1½ hours (20 minutes per 500 g/1 lb plus 20 minutes). Turn the bird every 20 minutes to brown evenly and 20 minutes before the end of cooking put the remaining mushrooms, whole, round

▶ A parsley mill can be used for any herbs, such as mint, tarragon or chives.

the bird to cook. When cooked, untie the chicken and put it on a heated plate garnished with the mushrooms. *Déglacer* the roasting tin with the port, check the seasoning, being generous with the pepper, and stir in the cream away from the heat. Serve this sauce in a gravy boat.

## Pigeons in red wine (pigeons en salmis)
*Time* 1½ hours
*Preparation* 30 minutes
*Cooking time* 8 minutes
*Serves* 4
The pigeons sold in France are usually younger and more tender than those on sale in other countries. This recipe is suitable for older birds requiring longer cooking.
1 large piece of pork skin
4 pigeons
100 ml (3½ fl oz) water
200 ml (7 fl oz) red wine
200 ml (7 fl oz) well-
    seasoned stock
bouquet garni
2 shallots *or* 50 g (2 oz)
    onion
2 cloves garlic
200 g (7 oz) mushrooms
25 g (1 oz) butter
25 g (1 oz) flour
salt, pepper
Cut the pork skin into 4 pieces and wrap each piece round a pigeon. Put them in an ovenproof dish with the water, and cook for 50 minutes in a moderate oven (190°C, 375°F/Gas 5). Then strip off the pork fat coating and remove the breast and legs from each pigeon. Put the carcasses in a saucepan with the wine, well-sea-

soned stock, bouquet garni, chopped shallots or onion and garlic and simmer for 20 minutes. Strain this stock and reserve. Gently fry the sliced mushrooms in the butter for 10 minutes, sprinkle the flour over, cook for another minute, then pour in the reserved stock. Stir well, check the seasoning and add the pigeon breasts and legs. Simmer for 8 minutes and serve very hot.

## Braised duck with green peas (caneton braisé aux petit pois)
*Time* 1 hour 20 minutes
*Preparation* 50 minutes
*Cooking time* 30 minutes
*Serves* 6
1½-kg (3-lb) duckling
salt, pepper
1 kg (2 lb) frozen peas
50 g (2 oz) unsmoked
    bacon
40 g (1½ oz) butter
a branch of savory *or* a
    bouquet garni
200 ml (7 fl oz) well-
    seasoned stock
25 (or 250 g/8 oz) small
    onions
10 ml (2 teaspoons) icing
    sugar
Wash the duck and pat it dry. Season the inside with salt and pepper, and prick the outside skin all over to allow the fat to escape. Roast it on a rack in a hot oven (200°C, 400°F/Gas 6) for 40 minutes. Defrost the peas, dip in boiling water and drain. Simmer the bacon in boiling water for 15 minutes, dice and fry in one-third of the butter. Assemble

the half-roasted duck, peas, bacon and savory or bouquet garni with the boiling stock in a casserole and cook in a moderate oven (190°C, 375°F/Gas 5) for 25 minutes. Meanwhile, peel the onions and cook whole with the rest of the butter, the sugar and 100 ml (3½ fl oz) water until all the water has evaporated and the butter and sugar are just turning brown. Add the onions to the duck and cook for another 5 minutes. Adjust the seasoning and remove the bouquet garni. Serve the duck surrounded by the peas and onions on a large plate.

## Roast goose (oie aux pruneaux)
*Time* 3 days
*Preparation* 55 minutes
*Cooking time* 2¼ hours
*Serves* 8
625 g (1¼ lb) prunes
600 ml (1 pint) red wine,
    preferably claret or
    Burgundy
1 small onion
4½-kg (9-lb) goose
30 g (1 oz) butter
45 ml (3 tablespoons)
    breadcrumbs
50 g (2 oz) liver pâté
pinch sage, crumbled
pinch *quatre-épices or*
    mixed spice
8 Golden Delicious apples
1 egg, beaten
50 g (2 oz) raisins
Soak the prunes for 48 hours in three-quarters of the wine. Then stone and stuff them, reserving the marinade.
    To make the stuffing, finely chop the onions and

the goose liver (stiffen the liver in the refrigerator beforehand), fry the onions in half the butter, then add the liver and fry for another minute. Take out the onions and liver and *déglacer* the pan with the rest of the wine. Add this gravy to the liver, then add the breadcrumbs, pâté, sage and spice and beat to a smooth paste. Stuff each prune with a little of this mixture and leave overnight. Before cooking the goose, remove the flights and any loose fat inside, and prick the skin of the breast and legs to allow the fat to escape easily during the cooking. Fill the inside of the bird with the prunes and sew up the opening. Put the goose in a roasting tin in a hot oven (210°C, 425°F/Gas 7) for 15 minutes. Then baste with 15 ml (1 tablespoon) boiling water and

▼ *Coq au vin.*

turn the goose on its side. Reduce the oven temperature to 190°C, 375°F/Gas 5 and continue turning and basting with boiling water every 20 minutes for 2 hours. Spoon off any excess fat. Half an hour before the end of the cooking, peel, core and dip the apples in beaten egg. Fill their centres with the raisins and a little nut of butter and put them to cook round the goose. When the goose is cooked, cut the cotton holding the vent together and lay it on a heated plate with the apples. Pour off the excess fat from the tin and *déglacer* with the reserved prune liquor. Season well and serve in a separate gravy bowl.

## Turkey stuffed with chestnuts (dinde farcie aux marrons)

*Time* 3 hours 40 minutes + overnight

*Preparation* 1½ hours
*Cooking time* 2 hours
*Serves* 6

3 chicken livers
30 ml (2 tablespoons) brandy
1 small onion
200 g (6 oz) raw ham
1 kg (2 lb) chestnuts
1 litre (1¾ pints) stock
100 g (3½ oz) cooked rice
salt, pepper
3-kg (6-lb) turkey
120 ml (8 tablespoons) oil
1 large sheet of pork fat

To make the stuffing, soak the livers in the brandy overnight, then chop finely with the onion and ham. Peel the chestnuts by making an incision in the top of each nut and boiling in water for 5 minutes. When peeled, cook in 750 ml (1¼ pints) stock for 30 minutes, then drain and chop coarsely. Mix with the chopped livers, onion, ham and rice. Season well.

Season the inside of the turkey and stuff it. Fasten the vent securely. In a large pan, brown the turkey on all sides in 45 ml (3 tablespoons) oil, then wrap it in the sheet of pork fat and tie carefully. Place in a roasting tin in a hot oven (210°C, 425°F/Gas 7) and spoon over the rest of the oil. Baste frequently during cooking; allow 20 minutes per 500 g (1 lb).

To serve, untie and remove the sheet of pork fat. Put the turkey on a heated plate and keep warm. Pour off most of the fat from the tin and *déglacer* with the remaining stock. Check the seasoning and serve this sauce in a gravy boat.

# Vegetables

The range of vegetables available in France is very wide, since almost every kind of vegetable can be grown there, and the quality is usually excellent. At the greengrocer's or in the market the French housewife expects to pick out her own fruit and vegetables individually from the displays. Vegetable dishes are often served by the French as a separate course and are not regarded simply as an accompaniment to a meat dish. For this reason, a great deal of care and attention goes into their preparation and cooking.

### Baked aubergines (aubergines à la provençale)

*Time* 2 hours 50 minutes
*Preparation* 20 minutes
*Cooking time* 1½ hours
*Serves* 6

500 g (1 lb) aubergines
salt
60 ml (4 tablespoons)
  olive oil
125 g (5 oz) chopped
  onions
600 ml (1 pint) stock
100 ml (3½ fl oz) tomato
  sauce (p. 87) *or* 100 ml
  (3½ fl oz) water and
  10 ml (2 teaspoons)
  tomato purée
30 ml (2 tablespoons)
  white wine
pepper
100 g (4 oz) grated cheese
  (Gruyère or Cheddar)

Cut the aubergines into 1-cm (½-in) slices, sprinkle with salt and leave to drain for an hour. Then rinse and pat dry. Fry the aubergines in a frying-pan with the oil, then fry the onions, adding more oil if necessary. Add the stock, tomato sauce, wine and pepper, but no salt. Simmer, uncovered, on a low heat for 1 hour. Remove to an ovenproof dish, cover with a layer of grated cheese, and bake in a moderate oven (190°C, 375°F/Gas 5) for 25 minutes.

### Braised beetroots and onions (betteraves aux oignons)

*Time* 20 minutes
*Preparation* 10 minutes
*Cooking time* 10 minutes
*Serves* 4

1 medium onion
75 g (3 oz) butter
500 g (1 lb) cooked
  beetroot, sliced
salt, pepper
100 ml (3½ fl oz) cream

Peel and chop the onions very finely. Heat the butter in a saucepan and gently fry the onion until transparent. Add the beetroot and leave to cook over a low heat for 10 minutes. Add salt and pepper, and a few minutes before serving stir in the cream. Do not let the cream boil.

### Broccoli with cream (brocolis au gratin)

*Time* 25 minutes
*Preparation* 15 minutes
*Cooking time* 10 minutes
*Serves* 4

750 g (1½ lb) broccoli
2 cloves garlic
salt

▼ Chopping an onion. Peel and slice off the top. Leave the bottom untrimmed. Stand the onion on its base and make a series of parallel cuts across the onion, followed by a second series of cuts at right angles to the first. Take care not to cut through the base. Turn the onion on its side and slice downwards through the cut section.

25 g (1 oz) butter
45 ml (3 tablespoons)
  cream
25 g (1 oz) breadcrumbs
  fried in 25 g (1 oz)
  butter
Wash and cook the broccoli with the garlic in boiling, salted water for 5 minutes. Drain and chop coarsely, but *do not mash*. Melt the butter in a saucepan. Put the broccoli in a buttered oven-proof dish, pour in the melted butter and stir in the cream. Season to taste and sprinkle the fried bread-crumbs over the top. Bake in a hot oven (200°C, 400°F/ Gas 6) for 10 minutes and serve.

## Braised carrots with cream
## (carottes à la crème)
*Time* 1 hour 15 minutes
*Preparation* 10 minutes
*Cooking time* 1 hour
*Serves* 4
750 g (1½ lb) new carrots
25 g (1 oz) butter
salt, pepper
300 ml (½ pint) chicken
  stock
1 egg yolk
60 ml (4 tablespoons)
  cream
chopped parsley
Scrape the carrots and cut them into 4-cm (2-in) lengths. Melt the butter in a saucepan and gently fry the carrots for a few minutes. Season lightly. Then add the stock, bring to the boil and cook uncovered over a mod-erate heat for 1 hour. To-wards the end, check that it does not burn, since all the stock should be absorbed.

Beat the egg and cream to-gether and, away from the heat, pour over the carrots. Do not allow to boil. Serve very hot, garnished with chopped parsley.

## Braised celeriac
## (céleri-rave à la grenobloise)
*Time* 50 minutes
*Preparation* 30 minutes
*Cooking time* 20 minutes
*Serves* 6
1 kg (2 lb) celeriac
juice of 1 lemon
2 cloves garlic
50 g (2 oz) butter
30 ml (2 tablespoons)
  chopped parsley and
  chives *or* just parsley
75 g (3 oz) grated cheese
  (Cheddar or Gruyère)
salt, pepper
150 ml (¼ pint) milk
Peel the celeriac and cut into thin slices. Cook in boil-ing, salted water with the lemon juice for 20 minutes and then drain well. Crush the garlic and beat it into the softened butter with the parsley and chives. Arrange a layer of the celeriac in a well - buttered ovenproof dish, cover with a little of the cheese, season and pour over a little milk. Repeat the layers until the dish is full, finishing with a layer of cheese. Dot with the garlic and herb butter and bake in a hot oven (200°C, 400°F/ Gas 6) for 20 minutes. Serve very hot.

## Stuffed mushrooms
## (champignons farcies)
*Time* 35 minutes
*Preparation* 20 minutes
*Cooking time* 15 minutes

*Serves* 4
350 g (12 oz) large
  mushrooms
*Stuffing:*
  50 g (2 oz) breadcrumbs
  50 g (2 oz) softened
    butter
  30 ml (2 tablespoons)
    chopped parsley
  3 cloves garlic, crushed
  50 g (2 oz) finely
    chopped onions
  salt, pepper
butter
Wipe the mushrooms and remove the stalks, keeping the tops whole. Mix to-gether the stuffing ingredi-ents, seasoning well, and add the mushroom stalks, chopped. Fill the mushroom tops with this mixture and arrange them on a well-buttered ovenproof plate. Bake in a moderate oven (190°C, 375°F/Gas 5) for 15 minutes.

## Brussels sprouts
## (choux de Bruxelles au beurre)
*Time* 40 minutes
*Preparation* 15 minutes
*Cooking time* 20 minutes
*Serves* 6
1·25 kg (2½ lb) brussels
  sprouts
salt
40 g (1½ oz) butter
This method of braising green vegetables in butter can be used for cabbage, spring cabbage or broccoli. Wash and trim the brussels sprouts. Cook in boiling, salted water for 8 minutes. Drain and put in the butter in a covered pan over a very low heat. Leave for 20 min-utes, shaking the pan from time to time.

▼ *Brocolis au beurre, petits pois au lard, carottes à la crème, aubergines à la provençale, ratatouille niçoise, la rapée.*

**Braised fennel (fenouils Riviera)**
*Time* 2 hours
*Preparation* 10 minutes
*Cooking time* 20 minutes
*Serves* 4

2 bulbs fennel
45 ml (3 tablespoons)
   olive oil
2 cloves garlic, chopped
100 ml (3½ fl oz) water
salt, pepper
15 ml (1 tablespoon)
   Pernod (optional)

45 ml (3 tablespoons)
  cream

Wash the fennel bulbs and cut in halves downwards. Put the oil, fennel, and chopped garlic in a pan with the water and a little salt and pepper. Cover the pan tightly and simmer for 1½ hours on a very low heat. After 1 hour add the Pernod. Then transfer the fennel to an ovenproof dish. Boil down the cooking juices. Stir in the cream away from the heat and adjust the seasoning. Pour this sauce over the fennel and cook in a moderate oven (180°C, 350°F/Gas 4) for 20 minutes.

## Green peas with bacon and onions (petits pois au lard)

*Time* 1 hour 5 minutes
*Preparation* 20 minutes
*Cooking time* 45 minutes
*Serves* 6

With the advent of the frozen pea, small fresh peas (*petits pois*) are increasingly hard to find in France, as elsewhere, unless you grow your own. However, if you can obtain some, this is the perfect dish for them.

1·5 kg (3 lb) fresh peas
100 g (4 oz) smoked
  bacon, in one piece
10 small onions
50 g (2 oz) butter
salt, pepper
10 ml (2 teaspoons) sugar

Shell the peas. Simmer the bacon in boiling water for 15 minutes, then drain and cut into cubes. Peel the onions, but leave whole. Melt the butter in a saucepan and fry the bacon dice gently; when they have changed colour add the peas, onions, salt and pepper. Cover closely and leave to cook for ¾ hour

on a very low heat. Just before serving add the sugar. Serve very hot.

## Casserole of potatoes with butter (pommes Anna)
*Time* 1½ hours
*Preparation* 15 minutes
*Cooking time* 1¼ hours
*Serves* 6
1 kg (2 lb) potatoes
salt, pepper
50 g (2 oz) butter
Peel and thinly slice the potatoes. Arrange in a well-buttered oven dish, adding salt, pepper and dots of butter to each layer of potato. Cover with greased paper and bake in a moderate oven (190°C, 375°F/Gas 5) for 1¼ hours.

## Duchesse potatoes (brioches en pommes de terre)
*Time* 1 hour 10 minutes
*Preparation* 30 minutes
*Cooking time* 20 minutes
*Serves* 4
1 kg (2 lb) potatoes
100 g (4 oz) butter
45 ml (3 tablespoons) cream
1 whole egg + 2 egg yolks
salt, pepper
grated nutmeg
Peel and cook the potatoes in boiling, salted water. Drain and dry over a low heat. *Mouli* or sieve and, while still hot, beat in the butter and cream, then the eggs, reserving a little egg for glazing. Season generously with salt, pepper and nutmeg, and beat hard to a smooth paste. Roll three-quarters of the mixture into 20 balls, then roll the re-maining quarter into 20 small balls and put them on top of the others. Glaze the *bri-oches* with the reserved egg and place on a greased oven sheet, not too close to-gether. Bake in a hot oven (200°C, 400°F/Gas 6) for 20 minutes. The *brioches* can be served with tomato sauce.

## Stuffed potatoes (pommes de terre provençale)
*Time* 1 hour 40 minutes
*Preparation* 20 minutes
*Cooking time* 15 minutes
*Serves* 4
This makes a good supper dish as well as a vegetable dish, though for the latter the amount of cheese could be decreased.
4 large soapy potatoes
1 large onion
1 green pepper
1 courgette
4 tomatoes
1 clove garlic, crushed
30 ml (2 tablespoons) olive oil
salt and cayenne pepper
100 g (4 oz) grated cheese (Gruyère or Cheddar)
25 g (1 oz) butter
Wash and bake the potatoes in their skins for 1¼ hours in a moderate oven (180°C, 350°F/Gas 4). Meanwhile, chop the onion and de-seed and slice the pepper. Slice the courgette without peel-ing it. Skin, quarter and de-seed the tomatoes. Fry the onion and courgette with the garlic in the oil, then add the pepper and tomatoes. Season to taste and cook over a low heat for 10 minutes.

When the potatoes are cooked, cut lengthways and scoop out the pulp without breaking the skins. Mix half the potato pulp with the other vegetables and refill the potato skins. Sprinkle with cheese and a little melted butter and return to the oven for another 15 min-utes, or put under the grill for 5 minutes.

## Potato cakes (galettes parmentier)
*Time* 1¼ hours
*Preparation* 40 minutes
*Cooking time* 20 minutes
*Serves* 8–10
2 kg (4 lb) floury potatoes
125 g (5 oz) butter
2 egg yolks
30 ml (2 tablespoons) ground almonds
3 portions *Petit Suisse*
15 ml (1 tablespoon) cream
15 ml (1 tablespoon) chopped parsley
freshly ground pepper
salt
15 ml (1 tablespoon) oil
Peel and boil the potatoes. Drain and dry over a low heat, then *mouli* or sieve while still hot. Beat 40 g (1½ oz) butter into the purée, and then the egg yolks, ground almonds, cheese, cream and chopped parsley. Beat to a smooth paste and season to taste. Roll out this dough to the thickness of 1 cm (½ in) on a floured board and cut into rounds with a pastry cutter. Fry the potato cakes in the remain-ing butter and the oil over a moderate heat, turning to brown both sides.

▶ Skinning a tomato. Dip the tomato in boiling water for about one minute. Then using a sharp knife pierce the skin and gently peel it off.

## New potatoes with garlic and herbs (pommes de terre estivales)

*Time* 1 hour
*Preparation* 20 minutes
*Cooking time* 35 minutes
*Serves* 4

1 kg (2 lb) small new
  potatoes
40 g (1½ oz) butter
15 ml (1 tablespoon) oil
15 ml (1 tablespoon)
  finely chopped shallots
  or onion
3 leaves mint, finely
  chopped
15 ml (1 tablespoon)
  parsley, chopped
2 cloves garlic, crushed
salt, pepper

Scrape the potatoes and bring them to the boil in a pan of cold, salted water, then drain at once. Melt the butter and oil in a frying-pan and fry the potatoes, with the pan covered, over a low heat for 20 minutes. Shake the pan from time to time. Add the shallots or onion, herbs and garlic, season with salt and pepper, cover and cook for another 15 minutes. Serve very hot.

## Burgundy potato cakes (la râpée)

*Time* 45 minutes
*Preparation* 20 minutes
*Cooking time* 20 minutes
*Serves* 4

1 egg
20 ml (1 heaped table-
  spoon) flour
15 ml (1 tablespoon)
  cream
350 g (12 oz) potatoes
100 ml (3½ fl oz) milk
salt, pepper
lard

Mix the egg, flour and cream into a thick batter. Peel the potatoes and grate on to a clean cloth. Leave to 'weep' for a few moments (they will change colour) then squeeze gently in the cloth and add to the batter. Dilute the mixture with the milk until it is like a pancake batter. Season well. Heat a frying-pan and fry the batter, as you would for pancakes, in the lard, allowing just enough to cover the bottom of the pan for each. Turn once to brown on both sides.

This quantity makes 4–5 pancakes of 20-cm (8-in) diameter.

## Ratatouille (ratatouille niçoise)

*Time* 1 hour 40 minutes
*Preparation* 1 hour 15 min-
  utes
*Cooking time* 20 minutes
*Serves* 4

1 aubergine
1 onion
1 pepper
1 courgette
4 tomatoes
60 ml (4 tablespoons)
  olive oil
1 clove garlic
bouquet garni
15 ml (1 tablespoon)
  chopped parsley
salt, pepper

Wash and slice the aubergine, without peeling, sprinkle with salt and leave to drain for an hour. Then rinse and pat dry. Slice the onion, de-seed the pepper and cut into slices. Wash and slice the courgette. Cut the tomatoes into quarters.

Fry the sliced pepper in the heated oil over a very high heat, then add the aubergines and courgette. Stir continually to prevent burning. Continue frying over a high heat and add the tomatoes, onion and crushed garlic. Season well and add the bouquet garni and chopped parsley. Cover and cook on a moderate heat for 20 minutes, stirring from time to time to prevent burning. There should be almost no liquid left when the cooking is finished. Remove the bouquet garni and check the seasoning before serving. Ratatouille can be served either hot or cold.

## Tomatoes stuffed with mushrooms (tomates farcies au maigre)
*Time* 1 hour 10 minutes
*Preparation* 35 minutes
*Cooking time* 30 minutes
*Serves* 6
6 large tomatoes
salt
50 g (2 oz) finely chopped onion
15 ml (1 tablespoon) oil
125 g (5 oz) mushrooms
50 g (2 oz) butter
pepper
breadcrumbs
Wash the tomatoes and slice off their tops. Spoon out their seeds and core without breaking the skins. Sprinkle in a little salt and leave them to stand. After about 30 minutes turn them upside down to drain. Meanwhile, chop the mushrooms and onions and gently fry them in the oil and half the butter until soft. Season to taste

with pepper. Fill the tomatoes with this stuffing and put a dot of butter on each. Cover the top with breadcrumbs, and cook on a well-greased ovenproof dish in a moderate oven (180°C, 350°F/Gas 4) for 30 minutes.

## Baked tomatoes (tomates à la provençale)
*Time* 30 minutes
*Preparation* 20 minutes
*Cooking time* 5 minutes
*Serves* 4
8 tomatoes
60 ml (4 tablespoons) olive oil
2 cloves garlic
parsley, chives and basil, chopped
30 ml (2 tablespoons) breadcrumbs
salt, pepper
Halve the tomatoes. Heat the oil in a frying-pan and fry the tomatoes, cut face down, for about 10 minutes over a gentle heat. While they are cooking, prick their skins. Then turn them over and continue frying over a low heat. When cooked, lift them out carefully and arrange on an ovenproof dish, cut faces up. Cover with a layer of chopped garlic, herbs and breadcrumbs, season well and pour the remaining juices from the pan over. Bake in a hot oven (200°C, 400°F/Gas 6) for 5 minutes.

## Ragoût of peppers (piperade à la basque)
*Time* 25 minutes
*Preparation* 10 minutes

*Cooking time* 15 minutes
*Serves* 4
1 onion
3 peppers
6 tomatoes
2 cloves garlic
15 g ($\frac{1}{2}$ oz) lard
branch of thyme
salt, pepper
4 slices fried gammon (optional)
4 fried eggs (optional)
Peel and chop the onions. De-seed and slice the peppers. De-seed and quarter the tomatoes. Fry the onions and crushed garlic in the lard over a high heat, then add the peppers. Fry these together for a few minutes, stirring all the time, then add the tomatoes, thyme and seasoning. Continue cooking and stirring for about 5 minutes.

To make the dish more substantial, lay slices of fried gammon on the piperade and top with fried eggs.

## Mushroom salad with a cream cheese dressing (salade de champignons)
*Time* 15 minutes
*Serves* 4
3 portions *Petit Suisse* or 45 ml (3 tablespoons) cream cheese
45 ml (3 tablespoons) milk
15 ml (1 tablespoon) chopped parsley
10 ml (2 teaspoons) chopped chives

▶ *Champignons farcies, nouilles and boeuf en daube.*

5 ml (1 teaspoon) French
mustard
juice of 1 lemon
200 g (7 oz) button
mushrooms
1 lettuce
4 tomatoes

Beat the cream cheese with
the milk, parsley, chives and
mustard. Add the lemon
juice, to taste. Wipe the
mushrooms and slice them
into this sauce. Serve on a
bed of lettuce and decorate
with quarters of tomatoes.

## Green salads

French lettuce salads are
often made with very coarse
lettuces which, if they are
well dressed, are delicious.
The simplest dressing is a
vinaigrette.

### Vinaigrette dressing
1 ml ($\frac{1}{4}$ teaspoon) French
mustard
15 ml (1 tablespoon) wine
vinegar
45 ml (3 tablespoons)
olive oil
salt, pepper

Mix the vinegar and mus-
tard together and slowly

beat in the oil, a little at a
time. Season to taste. Alternatively, omit the mustard
and beat the oil slowly into
the vinegar, a spoonful at a
time. Season with salt and
pepper to taste.

To dress a green salad,
rub a cut clove of garlic
around a salad bowl, then
tear into it some well-
washed and drained lettuce
leaves. Pour the vinaigrette
dressing over and turn it all
very carefully to make sure
the dressing is well distri-
buted.

Lettuce can also be mixed
with either of the following
dressings: mashed hard-
boiled egg yolk, orange juice
and basil; or 45 ml (3 tablespoons) cream mixed with
15 ml (1 tablespoon) lemon
juice, garnished with a little
thinly pared, finely chopped
lemon peel.

Endives can be mixed
with croûtons of fried bread
rubbed with garlic, or hard-
boiled egg and capers, or
very finely chopped spring
onions. Each of these salads
requires a vinaigrette dressing.

A watercress salad with

▲ For a good vinaigrette
dressing:
*A sage should add the salt,
a miser the vinegar, and a
spendthrift the oil.*
(Provençal proverb)

diced cheese, such as
Gruyère or Cheddar, can
have a lemon-and-oil dressing or a vinaigrette dressing.
Watercress can be mixed
with lettuce and dressed
with 45 ml (3 tablespoons)
cream to 15 ml (1 table-
spoon) wine vinegar and
sprinkled with paprika.

Sliced chicory can be
mixed with cooked beetroot,
tarragon and mayonnaise.
Or serve it with a dressing
made of grapefruit juice and
olive oil mixed with seg-
ments of orange cut into
thirds.

### Red cabbage salad
(salade cramoisie)
*Time* 10 minutes
*Serves* 4
heart of a good red
cabbage
25 g (1 oz) salted peanuts
vinaigrette dressing (p. 70)
2–4 hard-boiled eggs

Trim and shred the cabbage. Mix it with the peanuts and dress with the vinaigrette dressing. Garnish with the hard-boiled eggs cut into segments.

## Chick-pea salad
### (pois chiches en salade)
*Time* 27 hours
*Preparation* 30 minutes
*Cooking time* 1½–2 hours
*Serves* 4
250 g (8 oz) dried chick-peas
2 cloves garlic

250 g (8 oz) tomatoes
vinaigrette dressing
12 black olives
Soak the peas for 24 hours, changing the water from time to time. Drain and rinse and place in a pan of fresh cold water. Bring to the boil and simmer for 45 minutes. Drain. Place in a pan of fresh, salted water with a chopped clove of garlic. Simmer until soft (30–60 minutes). Drain and rub off the skins. (This is easier if they are put in a bowl of cold water.) Leave

to dry before using in the salad. Rub the inside of a salad bowl with the other clove of garlic and in it mix the peas with the quartered tomatoes. Dress with a well-seasoned vinaigrette dressing and garnish with black olives.

▼ A *salad composée* with hard-boiled eggs, tomatoes, Gruyère cheese, walnuts and lettuce, served with a vinaigrette dressing.

## Autumn salad
## (salade d'automne)
*Time* 40 minutes
*Serves* 6
500 g (1 lb) potatoes
1 bunch watercress
6 young sticks of celery
½ cucumber
75 g (3 oz) Gruyère or
    Cheddar cheese
75 g (3 oz) walnuts
15 ml (1 tablespoon) finely
    chopped onion
parsley and chives,
    chopped
vinaigrette dressing
Wash and boil the potatoes
in their skins in salted water.
When cooked, peel immedi-
ately and cut into dice. Wash
and pick over the watercress.
Wash and slice the celery
and cucumber. Cut the
cheese into cubes and
roughly chop the nuts. Line
a salad bowl with the watercress and mix all the other
ingredients in the middle.
Pour over a vinaigrette dressing and serve.

▼ Olive stoner and garlic
press.

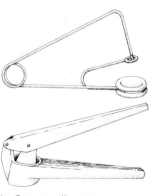

▶ *Coupes d'or aux
pamplemousses.*

## Red and green salad
## (salade vert et rouge)
*Time* 15 minutes
*Serves* 4
4 hard-boiled eggs
bunch of watercress
3 small cooked beetroots
8 anchovy fillets
10 ml (2 teaspoons) very
    finely chopped onion
vinaigrette dressing
chopped chives
Shell and cut the eggs into
halves. Wash and trim the
watercress. Peel and dice
the beetroot. Pile the beetroot in the centre of a plate
and surround with the watercress. Lay the eggs on the
watercress and decorate the
beetroot with the anchovies.
Mix the onion into the
vinaigrette dressing, pour
over the salad, sprinkle with
chopped chives and serve.

▲ *Salade niçoise* and *pois
chiches en salade.*

## Salad mimosa
## (salade mimosa)
*Time* 10 minutes
*Serves* 4
4 lettuce hearts
yolks of 4 hard-boiled eggs
45 ml (3 tablespoons)
    cream
15 ml (1 tablespoon)
    lemon juice
salt and white pepper
Wash the lettuce hearts carefully, but do not tear apart.
Dry well and put one on
each individual plate. Chop
the egg yolks very finely and
sprinkle them over the lettuces. Mix the cream and
lemon juice with a little salt
and pepper and pour over
the salads.

# Desserts

Many French people prefer to finish a meal with raw fruit and cheese rather than a sweet dessert. Desserts are therefore less essential to the structure of a French meal than the hors-d'oeuvre or soup. The French housewife prefers to buy expertly finished tarts and pastries from the shops rather than try to compete with the professionals. However, for those who have tasted these and wish to try making their own, here are some recipes for French fruit tarts and other sweets.

## Caramelizing
Time *20 minutes*
Place *25 g (1 oz) granulated sugar and 15 ml (1 tablespoon) water in a thick-bottomed pan over a low heat. Leave the syrup to boil until all the water has evaporated, without stirring or shaking the pan. Then stir while the sugar turns gold. Add 30 ml (2 tablespoons) water, a spoonful at a time, and mix well over a high heat. Pour into the bowl or mould to be coated. Turn the bowl round and round until the inside is completely covered. Leave to cool.*

## Honey cream
## (crème d'Homère)
*Time* 3½ hours
*Preparation* 15 minutes
*Cooking time* 45 minutes
*Serves* 4
sugar and water for
  caramelizing
150 ml (¼ pint) white wine
30 ml (2 tablespoons)
  clear honey
1 ml (¼ teaspoon)
  cinnamon
thinly pared rind of a small
  lemon
3 eggs
Coat a pudding basin with caramel. Put the wine, honey, cinnamon and lemon rind in an enamel or non-stick saucepan and simmer for 10 minutes, then strain. Beat the eggs and stir in the wine mixture. Pour the custard into the caramelized bowl and stand in a tin of water in a moderate oven (170°C, 325°F/Gas 3) for 40–45 minutes. Leave to get cold and turn out of the bowl

▲ A deep *bain-marie* pan and stand.

before serving. This custard can be made in small individual bowls, in which case cook for only 30 minutes in the oven.

## Lemon mousse
## (mousse au citron)
*Time* 4 hours 25 minutes
*Preparation* 25 minutes
*Chill* 4 hours
*Serves* 6
3 lemons
6 eggs
100 g (4 oz) castor sugar
Grate the rinds of 2 lemons and squeeze the juice from all 3. Separate the eggs. Beat the egg yolks with the grated rind, lemon juice and sugar and put them in to a saucepan. Stand the saucepan in a *bain-marie* and stir until the mixture is thick enough to coat the back of a spoon. Put aside to cool. Whisk the egg whites until they form peaks, then fold them into the lemon cream. Transfer to a serving bowl

and leave in the refrigerator for several hours until required. Serve very cold but not frozen.

## Chocolate mousse
## (mousse au chocolat)
*Time* 4 hours 20 minutes
*Preparation* 20 minutes
*Freeze* 4 hours
*Serves* 6
200 g (8 oz) plain
  chocolate
90 ml (6 tablespoons)
  strong black coffee
3 eggs
90 ml (6 tablespoons)
  sweetened condensed
  milk
Grate the chocolate into a saucepan and slowly melt with the coffee over a low heat, stirring occasionally to make a smooth cream. Beat the egg yolks and the condensed milk and then add the chocolate cream. Whip the egg whites until stiff and fold into the mixture of eggs and chocolate. Put into a serving bowl and freeze in the refrigerator for about 4 hours before serving.

## Orange soufflé
## (soufflé à l'orange)
*Time* 30 minutes
*Preparation* 15 minutes
*Cooking time* 12–15 minutes
*Serves* 4
4 large oranges
4 eggs
20 g (¾ oz) self-raising
  flour
100 g (4 oz) castor sugar
30 ml (2 tablespoons)
  Cointreau (optional)
icing sugar

25 ml (1½ tablespoons)
milk

Cut the oranges in halves.
Remove all the flesh, taking
care not to break the skins.
Liquidize the flesh for a
moment, then strain off the
juice, discarding the pulp.
Separate the eggs. Mix the
flour, sugar, 120 ml (8
tablespoons) orange juice
(or 90 ml/6 tablespoons if
using Cointreau), Cointreau,
milk and egg yolks in a bowl.
In a separate bowl, beat the
egg whites until they form
peaks, then fold them into
the orange mixture. Spoon
into the orange skins and
cook in a hot oven (210°C,
425°F/Gas 7) for 12–15
minutes. Serve immediately,
sprinkled with icing sugar.

## Grapefruit snow
## (coupes d'or aux
## pamplemousses)
*Time* 4 hours 25 minutes
*Preparation* 25 minutes
*Chill* 4 hours
*Serves* 4

2 grapefruit
100 g (4 oz) castor sugar
4 eggs
45 ml (3 tablespoons)
cream
grated rind of 1 lemon

Cut the grapefruit into halves
and remove the flesh without cutting through the
skins. Reserve the skins in
the refrigerator until needed.
Liquidize the flesh for a
moment and strain off the
juice, discarding the pulp.
Mix the juice with the sugar,
egg yolks, cream and grated
lemon rind in a saucepan.
Either cook gently over a low
heat, or in a *bain-marie*, stirring all the time, until the

mixture coats the back of a
spoon. Do not boil. Allow to
cool, then fold in the egg
whites, beaten stiffly, and
fill the grapefruit skins with
this mixture. Leave in the
refrigerator until required.
Serve very cold but not
frozen stiff.

## Coffee ice cream
## (glace au café)
*Time* 6½ hours
*Preparation* 25 minutes
*Freezing* 6 hours
*Serves* 4–6

200 ml (7 fl oz) double
cream
60 ml (4 tablespoons) milk
175 g (6 oz) sugar
6 egg yolks
15 ml (3 teaspoons) *very*
strong fresh black coffee
200 ml (7 fl oz) evaporated
milk chilled for 2 hours
before use

Mix the cream and milk together and beat until stiff.
Beat the sugar and egg yolks

together until the mixture is
light-coloured and thick.
Fold the cream into the eggs
and sugar and add the
coffee. Then beat the evaporated milk until stiff and
fold it into the egg mixture.
Spoon into a freezing con-
tainer and freeze for about 6
hours. This ice cream does
not freeze very hard and
needs very little time out of
the freezer before serving.

## Pineapple
## (ananas de minuit)
*Time* 1¼ hours
*Preparation* 10 minutes
*Serves* 6

1 good fresh pineapple
60 ml (4 tablespoons) gin
75 ml (5 tablespoons)
castor sugar
50 g (2 oz) toasted
almonds, chopped
vanilla ice cream (optional)

Cut the pineapple in halves
lengthways and scoop out
the flesh taking care not to

▼ Making a lemon mousse.
Fold beaten egg white into
a cream mixture with a
spatula or knife using a
figure of eight movement
across the bowl.

break the skin. Discard the hard core. Cut the flesh into 2-cm (1-in) cubes. Put the pineapple to soak for 1 hour with the gin and sugar. Keep the 2 shells in the refrigerator. Just before serving, put the pineapple back into the shells and sprinkle over them the toasted almonds. Alternatively, put a layer of vanilla ice cream in the bottoms of the pineapple shells and pile the pineapple on top. Decorate with the almonds.

## Pears in red wine
## (poires au vin rouge)
*Time* 3 hours 10 minutes
*Preparation* 10 minutes
*Cooking time* 1 hour
*Serves* 4
500 g (1 lb) small firm
  pears
300 g (10 oz) sugar
200 ml (7 fl oz) red wine,
  preferably Burgundy

1 clove
pinch cinnamon and grated
  nutmeg
Peel the pears but leave whole with their stalks on. Put them in an enamel or non-stick saucepan with the rest of the ingredients, cover and simmer over a low heat for about 1 hour. Turn the pears at intervals to ensure they are evenly cooked. Then arrange them in a bowl with their stalks upwards and pour the syrup over them. Serve cold.

▼ *Ananas de minuit,
coupes 'sevillanas',
profiteroles au chocolat,
tarte au citron* and *crème
patissière.*

## Winter fruit salad
## (coupes 'sevillanas')
*Time* 30 minutes + overnight
*Preparation* 30 minutes
*Serves* 6
50 g (2 oz) raisins
50 g (2 oz) dried figs
200 ml (7 fl oz) Madeira
  *or* medium-sweet sherry
5 good oranges
1 small pineapple
50 g (2 oz) fresh (or dried)
  dates
Soak the raisins and figs in the Madeira or sherry over-

night. The next day peel and remove all the white pith from the oranges and cut the segments into 2-cm (1-in) pieces. Peel and cut the pineapple into similar-sized pieces, discarding the hard core. Mix together the dates, stoned and cut into halves, the figs, cut into pieces, the oranges, pineapple and raisins with the marinating liquor. Leave in a cool place for several hours.

## Profiteroles (profiteroles au chocolat)

*Time* 2 hours 10 minutes
*Preparation* 40 minutes
*Cooking time* 40 minutes
*Serves* 4
choux pastry made with 2 eggs (p. 26)
10 ml (2 teaspoons) icing sugar
vanilla or coffee ice cream

*Chocolate sauce:*
50 g (2 oz) plain chocolate
15 ml (1 tablespoon) warm water
45 ml (3 tablespoons) double cream
15 g ($\frac{1}{2}$ oz) softened butter

Make the choux pastry as directed, but include 10 ml (2 teaspoons) icing sugar with the water and butter. Pipe the paste in 7-cm (3-in) well separated rounds on to a greased oven tray and bake in a hot oven (220°C, 425°F/Gas 7) for 30 minutes. If they start to brown too fast, turn down the oven to 190°C, 375°F/Gas 5 after 20 minutes. When cooked, make a slit in the side of each profiterole to allow the steam to escape and return to the oven, turned off and with the door slightly open,

for a further 10 minutes to dry out. Stand on a rack to cool.

Make the chocolate sauce by grating the chocolate into the water in a saucepan and gently melting it, stirring all the time. When it is smooth and creamy, remove from the heat and stir in first the cream, then the softened butter. Keep warm until needed.

To serve, put some ice cream in the centre of each profiterole, stand in individual bowls and pour over the chocolate sauce.

## Iced meringues (meringues glacées)

*Time* 6 hours 45 minutes
*Preparation* 15 minutes
*Cooking time* 2$\frac{1}{2}$ hours + 3 hours' chilling
*Serves* 6

150 g (6 oz) icing sugar
6 egg whites
20 ml (4 teaspoons) flour
150 g (6 oz) chopped nuts
(almonds, hazelnuts or
walnuts)

Sieve the sugar. Beat the egg whites until they form peaks, then beat in 60 ml (4 tablespoons) of the sugar. Fold in the remaining sugar, flour and nuts. Line 2 oven trays with well-oiled grease-proof paper and pipe on the meringues in well-spaced rounds about 8 cm (3 in) across. Bake in a cool oven (100°C, 200°F/Gas $\frac{1}{4}$) for about $2\frac{1}{2}$ hours. Leave to cool.

To serve, chill in the freezing compartment of the refrigerator for about 3 hours, then fill with coffee ice cream just before serving, sandwiching the meringues together in pairs.

## Chestnut Mont Blanc (marrons en Mont-Blanc)

*Time* 40 minutes

*Preparation* 40 minutes
*Serves* 6

250 g (8 oz) vanilla sugar
(p. 92) + extra 75 g
(3 oz) for whipped
cream (optional)
30 ml (2 tablespoons)
water
500-g (1-lb) can chestnut
purée, unsweetened
40 g (1$\frac{1}{2}$ oz) softened
butter
150 ml ($\frac{1}{4}$ pint) cream

Make a thick syrup with the 250 g (8 oz) sugar and water. Mix this syrup into the chestnut purée, then beat in the softened butter to make a smooth cream. Using an icing bag with a fine round nozzle, pipe a mound of 'vermicelli' on to a serving dish. Whip the cream, adding the extra vanilla sugar if desired. Pipe round the base of the chestnut mound, adding a crown on top. Alternatively, the chestnut purée can be piped into small boat-shaped pastry cases and decorated with a rosette of cream.

## Charlotte with mandarin oranges (charlotte aux oranges)

*Time* 7 hours
*Preparation* 45 minutes
*Chill* 6 hours
*Serves* 6

2 small cans mandarin
oranges
25 sponge fingers
15 ml (1 tablespoon)
cornflour
1 egg yolk
juice of 1 orange
juice of 1 lemon
75 g (3 oz) ground
almonds
60 ml (4 tablespoons) rum
or sherry
orange marmalade
walnuts for decoration

Drain the cans of oranges into 2 separate bowls. Crumble 5 sponge fingers. Mix the cornflour and egg in a saucepan with the orange and lemon juice. Beat hard and cook over a low heat until the mixture thickens. Add the biscuit crumbs, ground almonds and 1 bowl of oranges. Mix well. Sprinkle the rum or sherry over the remaining biscuits and line a charlotte mould with them. Spread a little marmalade over the biscuits in the bottom of the mould and cover with a layer of half the orange cream. Spread another thin layer of marmalade and then the rest of the cream. Use the remaining biscuits to cover the top of the mould. Chill until required, then unmould and decorate with the remaining oranges and the walnuts, halved.

Ideally, chill for at least 6 hours before serving.

## Lemon tart
## (tarte au citron)
*Time* 1 hour
*Preparation* 20 minutes
*Cooking time* 25–30 minutes
*Serves* at least 4
150 g (5 oz) shortcrust
    pastry
2 eggs
180 g (6 oz) castor sugar
2 lemons
60 g (2½ oz) melted butter
50 g (2 oz) flour
50 g (2 oz) ground
    almonds
a little egg white
*Garnish:*
2 lemons
Line an 18-cm (7-in) flan tin or ring with the pastry. Beat the eggs in a bowl, then add the sugar and the grated rinds and juice of 2 lemons. Beat well. Pour in the melted butter and stir in the flour and ground almonds. Paint the bottom of

▶ Making pâte sablée.

the pastry with a little beaten egg white and fill with the lemon mixture. Peel the 2 remaining lemons so all the pith is removed and then cut them into very thin slices with a sharp knife. Arrange them over the top of the pie. Bake for 25–30 minutes in a hot oven (220°C, 425°F/ Gas 7). Serve hot or cold.

## Strawberry tart
## (tarte sablée aux fraises)
*Time* 4 hours 5 minutes
*Preparation* 1¼ hours
*Cooking time* 20–25 minutes
*Serves* 6
*Sweet biscuit pastry:*
250 g (8 oz) flour
100 g (4 oz) butter,
    softened
1 egg

50 g (2 oz) castor sugar
pinch salt
300 ml (½ pint) cold
    confectioner's custard
    (p. 80).
500 g (1 lb) strawberries
45 ml (3 tablespoons)
    redcurrant jelly
15 ml (1 tablespoon) water
    or kirsch
To make the pastry, put the flour in a heap on a board and make a well in the centre. Put all the ingredients into the well, then, using the fingertips, work the butter and eggs together (see photograph below). Gradually take in the flour and continue working until you have a smooth dough. Knead for a few moments, then leave to rest in the refrigerator for an hour. Then roll out to ½ cm (¼ in) thick

and line a 20-cm (8-in) flan tin. Bake blind for 20–25 minutes in a moderate oven (180°C, 350°F/Gas 4). Remove from the tin and cool on a rack.

Just before serving, put the cold custard in the pastry case and arrange the strawberries in a single layer on top, very close together so that they completely cover the custard. Melt the redcurrant jelly with the water or kirsch and, using a brush, glaze the strawberries.

## Confectioner's custard (crème pâtissière)
*Time* 1 hour 20 minutes
*Preparation* 20 minutes
*Cooking time* 5 minutes
2 egg yolks
65 g (2½ oz) castor sugar
30 ml (2 tablespoons) flour
200 ml (7 fl oz) hot milk
Beat the egg yolks and sugar together, then add the flour and continue beating. Slowly pour in the hot milk, making sure it is well mixed with the eggs. Pour the custard into a saucepan and bring to the boil over a moderate heat. Continue cooking for a few minutes, stirring all the time. Remove from the heat and allow to cool before use.

## Rhubarb meringue tart (tarte à la rhubarbe meringuée)
*Time* 1½ hours
*Preparation* 1 hour
*Cooking time* 10 minutes
*Serves* 4
150 g (5 oz) shortcrust pastry
500 g (1 lb) rhubarb
250 g (8 oz) sugar
2 eggs
100 g (4 oz) icing sugar
Line an 18-cm (7-in) flan tin or ring with the pastry and bake blind in a hot oven (220°C, 425°F/Gas 7) for 20 minutes. Stew the rhubarb with the sugar but no water until soft—about 40 minutes. Leave the rhubarb to cool, then beat in the egg yolks and pour into the pastry case. Beat the egg whites until stiff and add the icing sugar. Beat again. Cover the rhubarb with the meringue and cook in a hot oven (220°C, 425°F/Gas 7) for 7–10 minutes. Serve hot or cold.

## Upside-down apple pie (tarte Tatin)
*Time* 2 hours
*Preparation* 30 minutes
*Cooking time* 20–25 minutes
*Serves* 4
50 g (2 oz) butter
150 g (5 oz) icing sugar
1 kg (2 lb) Golden Delicious apples
125 g (4 oz) puff pastry
egg yolk for glazing
Generously butter a 20-cm (8-in) sandwich tin and sprinkle the sugar over it. Peel, core and quarter the apples and arrange around the tin, just overlapping, in concentric rings. Dot on the rest of the butter and put on to a hotplate or gas ring. Watch over it very carefully to check that the sugar caramelizes evenly without

◀ Glazing a strawberry tart.

*▶ Poires au vin rouge.*

burning; if necessary, move the tin from side to side of the ring to obtain even browning. Leave to cool.

Roll out the puff pastry and cut it into a circle to fit the sandwich tin. Cover the apples with this pastry, glaze with the beaten egg yolk and bake in a hot oven (220°C, 425°F/Gas 7) for 20–25 minutes. Turn out and serve upside down with the apples on top.

## Apricot pie (tarte alsacienne aux abricots)

*Time* 2 hours 50 minutes
*Preparation* 15 minutes
*Cooking time* 30 minutes
*Serves* 6
250 g (8 oz) shortcrust pastry
750 g (1½ lb) fresh apricots
125 g (5 oz) castor sugar
50 g (2 oz) flour
2 eggs
100 ml (4 fl oz) cream

Line a 27-cm (10-in) flan dish with the shortcrust pastry. Wash and.cut the apricots into halves and re-move their stones. Arrange them, touching each other, in circles round the dish and sprinkle with 25 g (1 oz) of the castor sugar. Mix the flour and the remaining sugar in a bowl and work in the eggs. Then stir in the cream and pour this custard over the apricots. Bake in a hot oven (220°C, 425°F/ Gas 7) for 25–30 minutes. Serve cold.

## Rum and nut cake (gâteau aux noix et au rhum)

*Time* 3 hours 10 minutes
*Preparation* 25 minutes
*Cooking time* 40 minutes
*Serves* 4
150 g (5 oz) shortcrust pastry
2 eggs
125 g (4 oz) chopped walnuts (or walnuts and peanuts mixed)
125 g (4 oz) vanilla sugar (p. 92)
50 g (2 oz) melted butter
15 ml (1 tablespoon) cream
10 ml (2 teaspoons) apricot jam
15 ml (1 tablespoon) rum
*Rum icing:*
150 g (5 oz) icing sugar

30 ml (6 teaspoons) rum

Line an 18-cm (7-in) flan dish or ring with the pastry and bake blind in a hot oven (220°C, 425°F/Gas 7) for 15 minutes. Separate the eggs. Make a cream of the nuts, sugar, butter, cream, rum and egg yolks. Then beat the egg whites stiffly and fold them in. Spread a little apricot jam over the bottom of the flan case and pour in the nut cream. Bake in a moderate oven (180°C, 350°F/Gas 4) for 35–40 minutes. Leave to cool, then ice with the rum icing, made by boiling together the sugar and rum. Serve cold, dec-orated with rum-flavoured cream if liked.

# Sauces

Sauces have long been one of the hallmarks of
French restaurant cooking. The names of many
famous dishes come from the sauces that
accompany the meat or fish. Although these
traditional sauces have recently been joined by a
range of lighter and less fattening garnishes, the
white and brown roux and the liaison of egg yolks
and oil or butter are still essential to many French
dishes, in both restaurant and family cooking.

## Basic white sauce (sauce Béchamel)

*Time* 10 minutes
*Cooking time* 10 minutes
60 g (2¼ oz) butter
70 g (4½ tablespoons) flour
450 ml (¾ pint) cold milk *or* stock
salt and pepper to taste

Melt the butter and mix in the flour over a low heat (picture 1). Allow to cook for about 2 minutes, stirring all the time. Do not let it colour. Pour in all the cold milk or stock and beat vigorously over a high heat (fig. 2). When it boils, turn down the heat and boil gently for 4 minutes, beating all the time. Season to taste.

**Note** The amounts of flour and butter can be altered for various thicknesses of sauce. Use:

20 g (¾ oz) butter
23 g (4½ teaspoons) flour
450 ml (¾ pint) liquid
for a thin sauce; or
40 g (1½ oz) butter
45 g (3 tablespoons) flour

450 ml (¾ pint) liquid
for a medium pouring sauce;
or
60 g (2¼ oz) butter
70 g (4½ tablespoons) flour
450 ml (¾ pint) liquid
for a coating sauce; or
80 g (3 oz) butter
90 g (6 tablespoons) flour
450 ml (¾ pint) liquid
for a very thick sauce (for soufflés, etc.).

## Rich white sauce (sauce à la crème)

*Time* 20 minutes
*Preparation* 10 minutes
*Cooking time* 5 minutes
*Serves* 4
100 ml (3½ fl oz) double cream
2 egg yolks
450 ml (¾ pint) basic white sauce
25 g (1 oz) butter (optional)

Mix the cream and egg yolks in a basin, then slowly add the hot white sauce. Return to the saucepan and re-heat carefully, stirring all the time.

Check the seasoning before serving. Up to the given quantity of butter can be stirred in at the end of the cooking, but the sauce must not be heated after the addition of the butter.

Serve with eggs, fish or poultry and, without the addition of butter, as the sauce for vegetables *gratinées*.

## Rich white sauce with onions and mushrooms (sauce poulette)

*Time* 35 minutes
*Preparation* 20 minutes
*Cooking time* 5 minutes
*Serves* 4
10 small onions or 100 g (4 oz) chopped onion
100 g (4 oz) mushrooms
40 g (1½ oz) butter
450 g (¾ pint) basic white sauce made with chicken stock
2 egg yolks
100 ml (4 fl oz) cream
100 ml (4 fl oz) white wine
salt, pepper, lemon juice

Simmer the onions in boiling water for 5 minutes. Slice and gently stew the mushrooms in one-third of the butter until soft. Make a basic white sauce with chicken stock. Beat the egg yolks and cream together and add slowly to the sauce. Return to the heat and carefully stir in the wine. Drain the onions. Add the onions and mushrooms and simmer for 5 minutes. Adjust the

◀ Making white sauce.

seasoning with a few drops of lemon juice, salt and pepper. Away from the heat, stir in the remaining butter. Serve with boiled poultry, such as *poule béarnaise*, or boiled fish.

## Onion sauce
### (sauce soubise)
*Time* 55 minutes
*Preparation* 35 minutes
*Cooking time* 15 minutes
*Serves* 4
500 g (1 lb) onions
25 g (1 oz) butter
100 ml (4 fl oz) white wine
100 ml (4 fl oz) well-
  seasoned stock
450 ml ($\frac{3}{4}$ pint) basic white
  sauce made with 60 g
  ($2\frac{1}{4}$ oz) butter and 70 ml
  ($4\frac{1}{2}$ tablespoons) flour
100 ml (4 fl oz) double
  cream

▼ Grilled chicken with *sauce choron* and *choux de bruxelles au beurre*.

Peel and roughly chop the onions, and cook in boiling water for 10 minutes. Then drain and put with the butter, wine and stock to simmer for 20 minutes. Sieve or liquidize this mixture and stir it into the basic white sauce. Return to the pan and simmer for a further 15 minutes on a very low heat. Stir in the cream and check the seasoning before serving. Serve with eggs, poultry, veal, lamb or vegetables.

## White sauce with mussels
### (sauce aux moules)
*Time* 20 minutes
*Preparation* 10 minutes
*Cooking time* 10 minutes
*Serves* 4
450 ml ($\frac{3}{4}$ pint) basic white
  sauce made with 60 g
  ($2\frac{1}{4}$ oz) butter, 70 g
  ($4\frac{1}{2}$ tablespoons) flour
  and a white wine court-
  bouillon (p. 30)
1 litre (2 pints) prepared
  mussels (see p. 30)

2 egg yolks
60 ml (4 tablespoons)
  double cream
Make the thick white sauce and add the cooking liquor from the mussels. Stir until smooth and simmer for 5 minutes. Mix the eggs and cream and carefully add the sauce. Return to the pan and bring back to the boil, stirring all the time. Add the mussels and check the seasoning before serving.

Serve with white fish or with a *gratinée* of fish.

## Basic brown sauce
### (sauce brune)
*Time* 45 minutes
*Preparation* 15 minutes
*Cooking time* 30 minutes
*Serves* 4
100 g (4 oz) bacon, in one
  piece
50 g (2 oz) onions,
  chopped
40 g ($1\frac{1}{2}$ oz) lard *or*
  clarified butter
40 g ($1\frac{1}{2}$ oz) flour
600 ml (1 pint) stock

bouquet garni
salt, pepper
Simmer the bacon in water for 15 minutes, then drain and dice. Fry the bacon and onions in the lard or butter until browned. Then remove from the pan and cook the flour in the fat (picture 1), stirring all the time until golden brown. Pour in the stock and mix well. Return the onions and bacon to the pan (picture 2) with the bouquet garni and seasoning. Simmer over a low heat for 20 minutes, then strain (picture 3). Adjust the seasoning.

## Brown sauce with Madeira (sauce madère)
*Time* 55 minutes
*Preparation* 45 minutes
*Cooking time* 10 minutes
*Serves* 4
300 ml ($\frac{1}{2}$ pint) basic brown sauce
45 ml (3 tablespoons) dry Madeira
Simmer the brown sauce with 30 ml (2 tablespoons) Madeira for 10 minutes on a very low heat. Just before serving add the rest of the Madeira. Serve with fillet of beef, kidneys or grilled veal.

## Sauce Robert (sauce Robert)
*Time* 55 minutes
*Preparation* 45 minutes
*Cooking time* 10 minutes
*Serves* 4
50 g (2 oz) shallots *or* onion
15 g ($\frac{1}{2}$ oz) butter
100 ml (4 fl oz) white wine
300 ml ($\frac{1}{2}$ pint) basic

▶ Making a basic brown sauce.

brown sauce
5–10 ml (1–2 teaspoons) French mustard
15 ml (1 tablespoon) tomato purée
Chop the shallots or onion finely and fry in the butter in a small enamel or non-stick saucepan. Do not allow to brown. Add the wine and simmer for 15 minutes over a very low heat. Then stir this mixture into the brown sauce and simmer for a further 10 minutes. Before serving, stir in the mustard and tomato purée. Serve with roast or fried pork, grilled chicken or veal.

## Devilled sauce (sauce au diable)
*Time* 55 minutes
*Preparation* 45 minutes
*Cooking time* 10 minutes
*Serves* 4
50 g (2 oz shallots *or* onions
100 ml (4 fl oz) white wine
300 ml ($\frac{1}{2}$ pint) basic brown sauce
15 ml (1 tablespoon) chopped parsley and chives
cayenne pepper
Slice the shallots or onions and put them in an enamel or non-stick saucepan with the wine to reduce by half. Stir this mixture into the brown sauce and cook for a further 10 minutes. Before serving, add the chopped herbs and season well with cayenne pepper. Serve with grilled meat or poultry.

## Mayonnaise

*Time* 30 minutes
*Serves* 4
1 egg yolk*
200 ml (7 fl oz) oil*
30 ml (2 tablespoons)
  vinegar *or* lemon juice
salt, pepper
*at room temperature
Beat the egg yolk and then slowly drip in the oil, beating all the time (see photograph). When all the oil has been beaten in and the mixture is a smooth thick cream, add the vinegar or lemon juice and season to taste.

## Mayonnaise with capers and gherkins (mayonnaise verte)

*Time* 10 minutes
*Serves* 4
25 g (1 oz) pickled
  gherkins
30 ml (2 tablespoons)
  capers
200 ml (7 fl oz)
  mayonnaise
25 g (1 oz) cooked spinach
ground black pepper to
  taste
Chop the gherkins and capers together and mix into the mayonnaise. Liquidize or *mouli* the spinach. Then, in a clean cloth, squeeze very dry. Add the leaf pulp to the mayonnaise and mix in well. Season to taste.

Serve with cold salmon, eggs or in an hors-d'oeuvre.

## Garlic sauce from Provence (ailloli)

*Time* 35 minutes
*Serves* 2–3
4 cloves garlic
1 egg yolk

200 ml (7 fl oz) olive oil
warm water *or* lemon juice
salt
Crush the garlic cloves, preferably in a mortar, and beat in the egg yolk. Then, beating all the time, drip in the oil. When the oil is completely absorbed, thin with a few drops of warm water or lemon juice. This sauce should be very stiff when it is finished. Season to taste with salt.

Serve with cold boiled meats, fish or potatoes.

## Chilli-flavoured garlic mayonnaise (rouille)

*Time* 35 minutes
*Serves* 8
1 clove garlic
1 egg yolk
200 ml (7 fl oz) olive oil
5 ml (1 teaspoon) Tabasco
  sauce
15 ml (1 tablespoon)
  tomato purée
90 ml (6 tablespoons) fish
  soup
Crush the garlic and beat it into the egg yolk. Drip in the oil, beating all the time. Then stir in the Tabasco sauce

◀ Making mayonnaise.

and the tomato purée. Just before serving, add the hot fish soup. Serve with bouillabaisse (p. 30).

## Hollandaise sauce (sauce hollandaise)

*Time* about 20 minutes
*Serves* 4
100 g (4 oz) butter
2 egg yolks
15 ml (1 tablespoon)
  lemon juice
salt
Melt the butter. Put the egg yolks and lemon juice in a bowl in a *bain-marie* and beat hard until the eggs start to thicken. Then remove from the *bain-marie* and beat in the melted butter drop by drop, as for mayonnaise. Beat continuously while adding the butter. Add salt and a few drops of lemon juice to taste, and stand the sauce in a *bain-marie* until needed. *This sauce cannot be re-heated.*

## Orange-flavoured hollandaise (sauce maltaise)

*Time* 20 minutes
*Serves* 4
100 g (4 oz) butter
2 egg yolks
20 ml (1½ tablespoons)
  orange juice
a few drops lemon juice
grated rind of 1 orange
Make a hollandaise sauce substituting orange juice for lemon juice. When all the butter has been beaten in, adjust the flavour with a little lemon juice. Stir in the grated rind. Serve with asparagus or broccoli.

## Béarnaise sauce
## (sauce Béarnaise)
*Time* 40 minutes
*Serves* 4–6
15 ml (1 tablespoon)
  chopped shallot *or* onion
60 ml (4 tablespoons)
  wine vinegar
5 ml (1 teaspoon) dried
  tarragon
150 g (6 oz) butter
3 egg yolks
salt, pepper
30 ml (2 tablespoons)
  chopped parsley
Put the shallot or onion,
vinegar and tarragon in an
enamel or non-stick saucepan and reduce by half, then
strain. Leave to cool. Make
a hollandaise sauce, sub-
stituting the strained vinegar
reduction for the lemon
juice. Stir in the chopped
parsley and season before
serving. Stand in a *bain-
marie* until needed.
  Serve with grilled meats.

## Sauce choron
*Time* 40 minutes
*Serves* 4–6
sauce béarnaise, as above
30 ml (2 tablespoons)
  tomato purée
Make a béarnaise sauce as
above, omitting the chopped

▶ A shallow *bain-marie*
filled with hot water in
which the egg yolks and
lemon juice are beaten
during the first stage of
making an Hollandaise
sauce. It is also used for
keeping sauces and other
foods warm before serving.

parsley. While the sauce is
standing in the *bain-marie*,
slowly stir in the tomato
purée. Check the seasoning
before serving.
  Serve with *tournedos* or
grilled poultry or veal.

## Tomato sauce
## (coulis des tomates)
*Time* 55 minutes
*Preparation* 5 minutes
*Cooking time* 45 minutes
*Serves* 4
500 g (1 lb) tomatoes
1 small onion
2 cloves garlic
15 ml (1 tablespoon) olive
  oil
bouquet garni
salt, pepper and sugar to
  taste
Roughly chop the tomatoes,
onion and garlic. Cook in the
olive oil with the bouquet
garni over a very low heat
for about 45 minutes, by
which time the sauce should
be very thick. Put through a
sieve or *mouli* and season to
taste with salt, black pepper
and a little sugar.

## Beurre manié
*Time* 7 minutes
25 g (1 oz) butter
30 ml (2 tablespoons) flour
Beat the butter to a cream
and mix in the flour to make
a smooth paste. Use for
thickening gravies, soups
and sauces.

## Black butter sauce
## (beurre noir)
*Time* 5 minutes
*Serves* 4
100 g (4 oz) clarified
  butter
30 ml (2 tablespoons)
  chopped parsley
45 ml (3 tablespoons)
  vinegar
Melt the clarified butter in a
pan and continue heating
until it turns a golden brown,
then remove from the heat
and stir in the parsley. Tip
the butter into a warmed
serving dish. Pour the
vinegar into the pan, boil
rapidly for a few moments,
then stir it into the butter.
Season to taste. Keep warm
in a *bain-marie* until needed.
Serve with fish, chicken or
vegetables.

## Parsley butter
## (beurre maître d'hôtel)
*Time* 1 hour
*Preparation* 5 minutes
40 g (1½ oz) butter
30 ml (2 tablespoons)
  chopped parsley
a few drops of lemon juice
Cream the butter and beat in
the chopped parsley and the
lemon juice. Shape into a
roll and chill in the refrigerator. Cut into thin slices and
serve as a garnish to grilled
meats or fish.

# Menus and timetables

### Planning a French meal

These timetables are rough guides to the order in which the various jobs for the preparation of the suggested meals should be done and the amount of time to allot to each task. They do not specifically allow time for washing up, laying the table or pre-heating the oven, and cooks will no doubt adapt them to suit their own circumstances.

The number of diners suggested for each meal is based on the size of the main dish; some vegetable dishes may need adjustment.

### Menu 1: dinner for four

Lettuce soup (p. 24)
Grilled lamb chops with thyme (p. 44)
Tomatoes stuffed with mushrooms (p. 68)
New potatoes with garlic and herbs (p. 67)
Green salad (p. 70)
Strawberry tart (p. 79)

### Timetable

*Day before meal*
Make and bake blind pastry case
Make confectioner's custard
Make lettuce soup, but omit thickening with cream and egg
*2 hours before meal*
Scrape potatoes, boil and drain
Empty tomatoes and leave to drain
Prepare stuffing for tomatoes
Prepare herbs and garlic for potatoes
Prepare thyme and oil for chops

Make croûtons
Wash and dry salad greens
*1 hour before meal* ·
Fill tomatoes
Start frying potatoes
Finish strawberry tart
*30 minutes before meal*
Put tomatoes into oven
Rub flavoured oil on chops
Dress salad
Start cooking chops
Prepare egg liaison for soup
Re-heat soup, thicken and serve

### Menu 2: dinner for six

*Stuffed mushrooms* (p. 63)
*Beef casserole with red wine* (p. 40)
*Macaroni*
*Endive salad* (p. 70)
*Fruit and cheese*

### Timetable

*Day before meal*
Marinate beef
Make stuffing for mushrooms
*4½ hours before meal*
Assemble beef casserole and put into oven
Wash endive, fry croûtons and make vinaigrette dressing
Stuff mushrooms
*20 minutes before meal*
Cook macaroni
Put mushrooms into oven
Assemble salad

### Menu 3: dinner for four

*Salad niçoise* (p. 18)
*Rabbit with olives* (p. 47)
*Casserole of potatoes* (p. 66)
*Lemon mousse* (p. 74)
*Day before meal*
Make lemon mousse

La Véritable
CUISINE
de
FAMILLE

Par
Tante Marie

Seul ouvrage
contenant
500 MENUS
et la manière
d'utiliser
LES RESTES.

A. TARIDE Éditeur
18 & 20 Bᵈ Sᵗ Denis. PARIS. Xᵉ Aʳ.

*2 hours before meal*
Peel potatoes, slice and
   assemble in ovenproof dish
Prepare rabbit
Put rabbit on to cook
Put potatoes into oven
Hard-boil eggs for salad
Prepare and cook beans for
salad
*15 minutes before meal*
Assemble salad

## Menu 4: dinner for six
*Tomato soup from Périgord*
   (p. 23)
*Scallops in white wine* (p. 28)
*Ham in a pastry case* (p. 47)
*Duchesse potatoes* (p. 66)
*Brussels sprouts* (p. 63)
*Pineapple* (p. 75)
*2 nights before meal*
Soak ham
*Day before meal*
Boil ham
Make potato purée, add butter,
   cream and eggs and leave in
   cool place
Wash and trim brussels sprouts
Bake ham
Prepare scallops and fill
   scallop shells
*2 hours before meal*
Shape potato purée into
   *brioches* and glaze
Cut up pineapple and marinate
Carve ham and re-form in
   pastry case

Prepare tomatoes, garlic and
   onions for soup
Prepare tomato and mushrooms
   for gravy
*1 hour before meal*
Put ham into oven
Make soup, leave to cook
Make toast for soup
Boil brussels sprouts
Start gravy
Put potatoes into oven
Check ham
Put brussels sprouts to simmer
   in butter
Finish gravy, except for cream
Assemble pineapple and chill
Top scallops with cheese and
   breadcrumbs, put under grill
Finish soup and serve

## Menu 5: supper for four
*Onion soup* (p. 23)
*Ragoût of peppers* (p. 68)
*Yoghurt* (bought)
*30 minutes before meal*
Make onion soup and leave to
   cook
Prepare vegetables for ragoût

Grill ham
Cook ragoût
Fry eggs

▼ French bread does not keep
for a long time so freshly baked
loaves are bought every day.

# French wines

The standard of named French wines is very strictly controlled, with laws that stipulate the exact area in which grapes for a top-quality wine may be produced and in some cases the type of grape that may be used for it. The best and most expensive wines come into this category, known as *appellation contrôlée*. The next quality is that of the *vins délimités de qualité supérieure*, known as VDQS. The third quality, over which there is no such control, is that of the *vins ordinaires*, suppliers of which are obliged to indicate the alcoholic strength of the wine on the label.

Generally speaking, when you buy wine you get what you pay for, but this does not mean that many of the cheaper wines, the *vins ordinaires*, are not excellent to drink.

## What to drink with French family meals

It is generally accepted that certain types of wine go best with certain dishes. For example, red wine is usually drunk with red meat or game, white with fish. Rosé wines go well with the same types of dish that suit white wines. Where food has been cooked in wine, it is best to drink the same wine, or a similar type, with the dish.

Only for the most elaborate dinners are different wines served with each course. The French, dining *en famille*, will tend to drink one wine— usually red—throughout the meal. It is likely to be a French wine, but a German white wine may be drunk in place of, for example, an Alsatian wine, and an Italian red—similar to the wines of Languedoc—would make a good substitute for the home variety. It is worth remembering this when shopping for wine to drink with a French-style meal.

The table right gives suggestions for types of wine which might be drunk with various types of dish. They are arranged in ascending order of price, with the most expensive at the bottom.

## Ideal serving temperatures for wine

Champagne 5°C (40°F)
Alsace 5°C (40°F)
White Bordeaux 5°C (40°F)
Rosé 8°C (46°F)
White burgundy 10°C (50°F)
Red burgundy 15°C (60°F)
Bordeaux 18°C (65°F)
Red wines benefit from being decanted well before the meal, as this serves to aerate the wine and let it reach room temperature. It will need a chance to 'settle', however. Ideally, red wine should be decanted about 8 hours before being drunk. There is no need to decant white wine, but do remember to chill it well in advance of the meal. Many rosé wines are also best served chilled.

| | FISH, SEAFOOD | RED MEAT, e.g. beef, game | WHITE MEAT e.g. chicken | CHEESE | DESSERTS |
|---|---|---|---|---|---|
| TYPE | dry white | full-bodied red | light – red, white or rosé | white or red, depending on cheese | sweet or semi-sweet white |
| WHITE/ ROSÉ | Languedoc Anjou Graves Burgundy (e.g. Chablis) Champagne | | Cabernet rosé Alsace | white wines for light cheeses | Sauternes Vouvray Muscat Champagne or continue drinking |
| RED | | Languedoc Corbières Beaujolais Côtes-du-Rhône Burgundy (e.g. Chambertin) Bordeaux | Médoc Bordeaux (e.g. St Emilion) | red wines for strong cheeses | wine that accompanied main course |

# Measurements

In this book, quantities are expressed in both imperial and metric units. The following tables summarize the equivalents used. The arithmetical correspondence is rarely exact, so in any one recipe follow either the metric or the imperial quantities: do not mix them.

**Solid measure**

25 g = 1 oz
100 g = 4 oz
250 g = 8 oz
500 g = 1 lb
1 kg = 2 lb
1 rounded tablespoon of unsifted flour = 15 g ($\frac{1}{2}$ oz)

**Liquid measure**

100 ml = 4 fl oz
200 ml = $\frac{1}{3}$ pint
300 ml = $\frac{1}{2}$ pint
400 ml = $\frac{2}{3}$ pint
450 ml = $\frac{3}{4}$ pint
600 ml = 1 pint

1 litre = $1\frac{3}{4}$ pints
1 teaspoon = 5 ml
1 tablespoon = 15 ml

# Book list

**French Provincial Cooking,** Elizabeth David, Michael Joseph, 1960, £10, Penguin, 1978, £1·25.
Far more than just a collection of recipes, this is an absorbing account of the cooking and eating habits of the French countryside.

**Charcuterie and French Pork Cookery,** Jane Grigson, Penguin, 1970, 95p.
A mine of information.

**Mastering the Art of French Cooking,** 2 volumes, Simone Beck, Louisette Bertholle, Julia Childe, Penguin, 1966, 1978, £1·95 each.
These books explain, with great clarity and attention to detail, how to cook French dishes.

**New Larousse Gastronomique,** Hamlyn, 1977, £10.
A complete compendium of world cooking with a strong French bias.

**The Cooking of Provincial France,** Time-Life, 1970, £6·95.
A lavishly illustrated cookbook.

**La Cuisine pour tous,** Ginette Mathiot, Livre de Poche, 1955.

**La Patisserie pour tous,** Ginette Mathiot, Livre de Poche, 1938.
Reliable and comprehensive French family cookbooks.

**Good French Cooking,** Mapie, Comtesse Guy de Toulouse-Lautrec, Hamlyn, 1966, £3·95.
A translation of the classic French work La Cuisine de Mapie, this is a reliable recipe book with a lot of character. Many of the recipes are from the South.

# Glossary

## English cooking terms and French equivalents

**Bake blind** (*cuire à blanc*): to pre-cook empty pastry cases, lined with greaseproof paper and dry (baking) beans to hold the pastry in shape.

**Baste** (*arroser*): to spoon hot fat or liquid over food, usually meat, while it is cooking, in order to prevent drying out.

**Blanch** (*blanchir*): to place vegetables or other foods in boiling water for a short time to remove any strong taste, to soften, to preserve colour (e.g. before freezing) or to make it easier to remove the skins.

**Blend** (*mélanger*): to mix together a dry and a liquid substance.

**Charlotte mould** (*moule à charlotte*): a flat-bottomed basin that can be lined easily with fingers of bread or biscuits.

**Clarified butter**: butter which has been slowly melted and strained to remove the moisture and impurities. This prevents the butter burning when it is used for frying.

**Dice** (*couper en dès*): to cut food into small cubes.

**Flights** (*ailerons*): the wing ends on poultry.

**Garnish** (*garnir*): to add an edible decoration to a dish just before serving, in order to improve its appearance and/or flavour.

**Glaze** (*glacer*): (1) to paint egg and water over pastry or dough before cooking so that it will shine when cooked; (2) to paint a thin layer of jelly over cooked fruit or meat to make it shine; (3) to dip glacé fruits in a thick sugar syrup in order to coat them.

**Lard** (*larder*): to thread strips of fat (*lardons*) through lean meat.

**Liaison** (*liaison*): thickening or binding of soup or sauce by the use of (1) egg yolks or (2) starch.

**Marinate** (*mariner*): to soak meat or fish in liquid (often wine) and flavourings before cooking in order to tenderize and improve the flavour.

**Mouli** (*mouliner*): to put through a vegetable mill or *mouli*. See *mouli-légumes*.

**Poach** (*pocher*): to cook food in liquid that is barely boiling.

**Purée** (*purée*): a smooth pulp obtained by passing food through a sieve, liquidizer or *mouli*.

**Reduce** (*réduire*): to boil a liquid in order to reduce its volume and so increase its flavour.

**Refresh** (*rafraîchir*): to dip hot food into cold water to stop the cooking process and cool it quickly.

**Sauté** (*sauter*): to brown food quickly in hot fat, either to cook it completely or just to seal it.

**Simmer** (*mijoter*): to cook food in a liquid below boiling point on a very low heat, so that the water shimmers but does not bubble.

**Vanilla sugar**: many recipes for desserts specify vanilla-flavoured sugar, and vanilla essence is a crude substitute for it. It is possible, though expensive, to buy vanilla sugar, but it is very simple to make at home. A vanilla pod in a tightly lidded jar of castor sugar will last for years. Each time some sugar is taken out it should be replaced with fresh.

## French cooking terms

**Agneau**: lamb.

**Aiglefin**: haddock.

**Ail**: garlic.

**Ananas**: pineapple.

**Andouilles**: black-skinned sausages, made with tripe, which are sliced and eaten cold.

**Artichaut**: globe artichoke.

**Baguette**: a long, thin loaf of white bread weighing 250 g ($\frac{1}{2}$ lb).

**Bain-marie**: 1. a deep pan filled with simmering water within which sits a bowl, often on a stand (p. 74). Its purpose is to cook food as gently as possible, e.g. egg mixtures which might otherwise curdle. 2. a shallow pan filled with hot water in which bowls or saucepans can be stood to keep foods and sauces hot (p. 87).

**Ballotine**: a galantine: meat or poultry which has been boned, chopped and returned to its skin, which is then tied in the shape of a small balloon and cooked; it is eaten cold and sliced.

**Beurre manié**: a mixture of butter and flour used to thicken soups and sauces just before serving.

**Boeuf**: beef.

**Bouillabaisse**: a substantial fish soup from Marseilles and Sète, made from Mediterranean fish and shellfish.

**Bouquet garni**: a bunch of herbs—typically, parsley, thyme and bay leaf—used for flavouring savoury dishes.

**Bourride**: a Provençal fish soup that is served with a garlic mayonnaise.

**Brioche**: a bun, made with rich dough that includes eggs, often incorporating a savoury filling.

**Canard**: duck.

**Caneton**: duckling.

**Cassoulet**: a casserole of beans containing *confit d'oie*

and pork or mutton. A
Languedoc dish.
**Charcuterie:** pork butcher's
and delicatessen.
**Charcutier:** a pork butcher.
**Chicorée:** endive.
**Chou:** cabbage.
**Chou-fleur:** cauliflower.
**Chou-rouge:** red cabbage.
**Choux de Bruxelles:** brussels
sprouts.
**Ciboulette:** chives.
**Confits d'oie:** joints of goose
cooked and preserved in goose
fat.
**Consommé:** a clear soup with
a meat stock base, usually with
a vegetable or pasta garnish.
**Coquilles:** scallop shells.
**Coquilles St Jacques:**
scallops.
**Court-bouillon:** a stock
made with vegetables and
often wine or vinegar, for
cooking fish.
**Crème pâtissière:** confectioner's custard: custard
cream used for French sweet
dishes, including pastries and
ice creams.
**Croissant:** a crescent-shaped
roll of rich, flaky bread.
**Croûton:** a small cube of
fried bread used as a garnish
for soups and stews.
**Daube:** stew or braise.
**Déglacer:** to clean with a
liquid (often wine) a pan in
which meat has been cooked;
the flavoured liquid is used as
a sauce or gravy.
**Déjeuner:** lunch; *petit
déjeuner*, breakfast.
**Dîner:** dinner or main meal.

**Endive:** chicory.
**Estragon:** tarragon.
**Etuver:** to stew.
**Extra vierge:** first pressing
(of olive oil).
**Farci:** stuffed.
**Fines herbes:** a mixture of
herbs—typically, parsley,
chives and tarragon.
**Graisse d'oie:** goose fat.
**Gratiner:** to brown the top of
a dish; *au gratin*, coated in a
sauce, sprinkled with breadcrumbs and/or cheese, and
browned either under the grill
or in the oven.
**Gros pain:** a long, white
French loaf weighing 400 g
(14 oz).
**Haute cuisine:** the lavish
cooking style of the French
aristocracy that now survives
in specialist restaurants all
over the world.
**Jambon:** ham.
**Lard:** bacon.
**Lard de poitrine:** either
salted or smoked belly of pork.
**Lardons:** strips of fat for
larding lean meat.
**Laurier (feuilles de):** bay
(leaves).
**Morue:** dry salt cod, sometimes called stockfish.
**Mouli-légumes:** a vegetable
mill.
**Mouliner:** to *mouli*, or pass
through a vegetable mill.
**Mouton:** mutton.
**Pain:** bread: *de campagne*,
coarse white; *complet*, wholemeal; *de seigle*, rye.
**Pâte:** pastry; *à choux*, choux
pastry; *à frire*, batter for

frying; *brisée*, shortcrust pastry;
*feuilletée*, puff pastry; *sablée*,
sweet biscuit pastry; *sucrée*,
sweetened shortcrust pastry.
**Pâté:** originally a meat pie,
now any meat loaf. Inter-
changeable with terrine.
**Pâtisserie:** cake shop; also,
food items sold therein.
**Petit déjeuner:** see *déjeuner.*
**Persil:** parsley.
**Poisson:** fish.
**Poivre:** pepper.
**Poivron:** pepper or capsicum:
*rouge*, sweet red; *vert*, green.
**Pomme:** apple.
**Pomme de terre:** potato,
sometimes abbreviated to
*'pomme'*, as in *pommes frites.*
**Porc:** pork.
**Potage:** a thick soup, often
made with a purée of
vegetables.
**Poule:** boiling fowl.
**Poulet:** chicken (usually
roasting).
**Poussin:** very young chicken,
4–6 weeks old.
**Quiche:** savoury tart.
**Ragoût:** stew.
**Rillettes:** a form of shredded
meat, usually made from pork.
**Roux:** a blend of melted
butter or other fat and flour:
the thickening medium for
many sauces.
**Soupe:** thick soup, often a
peasant recipe.
**Souper:** supper.
**Terrine:** originally a form of
meat loaf cooked in an
earthenware bowl, but now
indistinguishable from pâté.
**Thym:** thyme.
**Veau:** veal.
**Vinaigrette:** an oil and
vinegar dressing.
**Vin:** wine; *blanc*, white; *rosé*,
pink (made from special grapes
—*not* a mixture of red and
white); *rouge*, red.
**Zest:** outer (coloured) layer of
the skin of citrus fruit.

◀ Gratin dish.

# Index

# Credits

## Artists
Gordon Cramp
Carol Folke
Kim Lane/Zip Art
Vanessa Luff
Peter Watson

## Photographs
Douglas Dickins, 2, 5, 10
French Government Tourist
  Office, 4

Denis Hughes-Gilbey, 16, 17,
  71
Mike Newton, 11, 19, 21, 23,
  25, 26, 28, 31, 32, 33, 34,
  35, 37, 39, 44, 45, 47, 48-9,
  54, 55, 56, 57, 60, 62, 64-5,
  67, 69, 72, 73, 75, 76-7, 78,
  79, 80, 81, 82, 83, 84, 86,
  87
Phoebus Publishing, 52
Shaun Skelly, 29, 61
John Topham, 10, 13
Tessa Traeger, 41
John Watney, 10
Crockery and other equipment
used in the photographs kindly

lent by P. S. Birrel, Copco
Cast-iron Ware, Cucina,
Richard Dare, Dartington
Glass Limited, Elizabeth David
Limited, Denby Tableware
Limited, Myriad Antiques.
Food prepared by Rhonda
Wraith.

## Cover
Photograph: Tessa Traeger
Painting: 'Luncheon of the
Boating Party' by Renoir,
reproduced by kind permission
of the Phillips Collection,
Washington D.C.